The Unintentional Advocate

Jerold E. Rothkoff, Esq.

ISBN: 9781790187386
Cover Image: Adobe Stock | Cover Design: Kristin Kane Ford

DEDICATION

To my wife, Erica, and our children, Liza, Julia, Evan, Greg, and Aitan, who give me their unwavering support and always push me to be the best person I can be.

TABLE OF CONTENTS

Preface

PREFACE

Initially, I did not decide to dedicate my law career to helping seniors and those with disabilities because I had a particular fondness for the elderly. Initially, I saw elder law as a means to make a living by practicing in an area of law that I thought had the capacity for an increased need over the years. However, what initially started as a means to support my growing family, has blossomed into my professional passion. As such, the unintentional advocate.

As I look back, I am reminded of the events that forever altered the course of my professional career. For the first 5 ½ years of my career, I had been practicing in the area of general civil litigation, with an emphasis in creditor's rights and personal injury law, when I became involved in an elder law matter.

The matter involved a spouse being sued for her husband's alleged outstanding nursing home bills. As I began to investigate the case, I became aware that I needed to become much more familiar with Medicaid and nursing home laws in order to provide the proper representation for my client. Coincidentally, I subsequently learned that the National Academy of Elder Law Attorneys was having its annual 1999 spring conference in Philadelphia. Within the first two hours at the conference, I became energized in a way that had eluded me my first years in the practice of law. Upon returning home that night (since the conference was local), I advised my wife that I wanted to change my practice area. I knew back then that there was something about this field of elder law that would fulfill me in ways which I never could have imagined when I went to law school and set out upon my journey to become a lawyer. Two hours at the conference changed my life.

One early case that I handled left an indelible impression on me and characterizes the essence of what elder law attorneys do for their clients. It involved a woman who suffered from Chronic Obstructive Pulmonary Disease (COPD). Medicare denied her coverage for a procedure called Lung Volume Reduction Surgery. At that time, in order for Medicare to pay for the complicated and risky surgery, the patient must have enrolled in a national trial program under Medicare. Once enrolled in the trial program, ½ of the patients received the surgery, the remaining ½ were randomized for continued therapy, which, in essence, was a death sentence. My client was randomized for continued therapy, and therefore Medicare would not cover the cost of the approximate $50,000 surgery. She did not have the financial means to pay privately for the surgery, and therefore, on her behalf, I appealed Medicare's denial. Through my research and investigation, I learned of a world-renowned cardiothoracic surgeon in St. Louis, MO who pioneered lung volume reduction surgery. With his assistance, my client won the administrative hearing, meaning that Medicare would cover the client's surgery. There were no words for the gratification I felt when I was able to explain to this family that I could help them. It is a feeling that I never will forget. My client and her family thanked me stating that she can now dream of the possibility of playing with her grandchildren for the first time, something that she could previously not have done due to her breathing difficulties. For the first time in my career I felt that I had a real impact on a family that was confronted with real problems. In an instant, life meant something more to me. I had become a problem-solver, and it felt good. It still feels good today.

Like almost every elder law attorney twenty years ago, I thought elder law was about protecting assets from the nursing home, drafting estate planning documents, and guardianships. Over the years, I have learned how narrow minded my views actually were.

Clients and their caregivers were coming to our office with typically more pressing issues than simply "protecting their money." Issues such as how to convince dad to leave the home to keep him safe, how to best take away dad's car keys, and how therapy can be maximized under insurance coverage. I realized I needed to do better to truly address our clients ever-increasing concerns.

In 2005, our firm, Rothkoff Law Group, adopted the "Life Care Planning" practice model by incorporating social work to assist families in advocacy for their loved ones. Life Care Planning has enabled us to truly provide "holistic" services that our clients need and deserve. Over the years, we have expanded our services to include Veterans benefits, client education programs, assisting clients with the increasing complexity of coordinating Medicare and other health insurance benefits for maximum coverage, and additional advocacy in a home and community setting. Thus, for the past several years we have been counseling clients and their caregivers on public benefits, veteran benefits, estate, tax, long term care, care coordination, health insurance, disability planning, and many more services not found in a traditional elder law firm.

I want to thank our dedicated elder care law team at Rothkoff Law Group for their commitment to improving the lives of seniors, those with disabilities, and their loved ones.

As I look back on these past twenty years, I have probably learned more from my clients than they have learned from me. The most important thing I have learned is to listen. Listen to the clients' wonderful stories about the wars they have fought, the places they have been, and the people they have met. We have much to learn from the elderly and disabled, and they have much to share. It has been an honor and privilege assisting seniors, the disabled, and their families. It is a debt of gratitude that I can only hope to repay.

LONG TERM CARE, ELDER CARE & LIFE CARE PLANNING

-1-

THE BENEFITS OF HAVING A CARE COORDINATOR ON YOUR SIDE

Rothkoff Law Group follows a unique elder law firm model called Life Care Planning (find out more at lcplfa.org). This model encourages its law firms to hire Care Coordinators (usually a social worker or nurse) to help clients navigate the long-term care maze. We often hear, "What does the care coordinator do?"

Meet your Caregiver Guide, Janie

When we tell folks that our firm has three social workers on staff, the reaction is either delight or confusion (or sometimes both). Below is an example of a typical client of **Rothkoff Law Group** (no actual confidential information is being shared).

Mr. and Mrs. Jones have been married since 1952. They have two adult children and still live in their home of 30 years. For the past six years, Mrs. Jones has been the primary caregiver of Mr. Jones who is living with dementia. Mr. Jones does not have any other medical issues other than moderate stage Alzheimer's. Mrs. Jones, however, has diabetes, hypertension, asthma, two bad knees and is overweight. Their daughter, Monica, comes by to help her parents, but she works full-time and has three school-aged children. The Jones' son lives out-of-state.

Mrs. Jones, faced with deteriorating health and the exhaustion of being a full-time caregiver for her husband, has begun seeking options for long-term care. Taking this step was difficult for Mrs. Jones, as she realized that their monthly income of $3,400 would not pay for very much and that their assets, the value of their home and $98,000 in cash, would be depleted very quickly.

Mrs. Jones and her children met with our office. At the meeting Mrs. Jones and her children learned about the VA Aid and Attendance Benefit that can be added to their monthly income of $3,400, bringing them up to around $5,400 a month. They also learned the importance of getting Mr. and Mrs. Jones' powers of attorney, advance directives and wills updated. After they decided to retain us, the Rothkoff team got busy. Our VA specialist, Joanne Solometo, started working on the VA application. An appointment was also established to meet Mr. and Mrs. Jones in their home.

In the home, Janie DeLeon Male, our Director of Care Coordination, set about to do the following list of items for the Jones family:

1. Assess Mr. and Mrs. Jones in their home for safety issues (recommend a shower chair, pull-down shower head, removing items off the floor, etc.) ;
2. Screen both Mr. And Mrs. Jones for depression;
3. Assist in getting the powers of attorney, advance directive, the wills, and VA application signed at their home so that Mr. Jones would not have to travel to an unfamiliar place;
4. Educate Mrs. Jones on UTIs, medication management, caregiver stress, hospice and long-term care options;
5. Offer referrals to various doctors such as geriatricians, geriatric psychiatrists, podiatrists and eye doctors as appropriate;
6. Explore the options for getting some help in the home to assist with caring for Mr. Jones;
7. Explore the idea of assisted living care for Mr. Jones, including using day care or respite care in an assisted living community;
8. Encourage Mrs. Jones to seek support through support groups or individual therapy from a Medicare provider.

After accomplishing the above issues, all recommendations and referrals were shared with both Mrs. Jones and her children. The family set about touring assisted living communities and interviewing home care companies. Two months later, however, Mrs. Jones suffered a major stroke. The daughter asked a neighbor to watch dad and went to the ER with mom. Mrs. Jones was admitted to the hospital for an undetermined length of time. The daughter, Monica, called us the next day and Janie responded with the following actions:

1. Called one of the assisted living communities the family had toured to discuss immediate placement in a memory care unit for respite care for Mr. Jones;
2. Connected the daughter and the community relations person after preparing the daughter for the admission process;
3. Educated the daughter on several topics concerning her mother, including confusion/disorientation during the hospital stay and the process of choosing and entering a rehabilitation facility; Provided on-going phone and email support to the daughter throughout this period;
4. Visited dad at the assisted living, consulting with their nurse about Mr. Jones' adjustment to the community;
5. Attended the father's care plan meeting at the rehab facility.

Mrs. Jones stayed in rehab for 52 days. At that time a decision had to be made as to whether Mrs. Jones could go home, move to assisted living or stay in the nursing home for long-term care. Monica called Dawn to discuss the situation.

Janie's role then:

1. Janie went with Monica to the next care plan meeting to gather the facts on Mrs. Jones. It was determined that due to immobility issues and other medical conditions Mrs. Jones would need to stay in the nursing facility for long-term care. The nursing home agreed to keep Mrs. Jones.
2. Janie then educated and discussed with the daughter how to be an advocate for her mother and father including attending care plan meetings, following the chain of command in each facility, getting to

know the caregivers, etc.

3. Janie reminded the daughter to contact our office if she has any questions or if she feels that after advocating for her parents she needs some additional support from the care coordinator.

Meanwhile, our office continued to file for Veterans Benefits for Mr. Jones and began a nursing home Medicaid application for Mrs. Jones, involving our Medicaid specialist, Alicia Kagan. We also reviewed Mr. And Mrs. Jones health insurance through our health insurance specialist.

In the end, this family, like so many clients, started off on one track to meet their father's needs and ended up needing a different plan to help both mom and dad. We were able to provide them with guidance and support throughout the changes, employing all members of our team. The care coordinator played a significant role in helping this family navigate the long-term care world, sticking with them through each transition.

2

LIFE CARE PLANNING:
WHEN YOU NEED TO KNOW THE WAY

"I need to come in right away," Susan told our office. Her mother, Florence, has cerebral palsy and her father, Maurice, who had been caring for her mother in their home, had a stroke and was undergoing rehabilitation at the hospital. Susan had hired round-the-clock caregivers for her mother and it was costing a fortune. She did not think the money would last for very long and she did not know what to do. Should her parents live with her? Susan investigated putting an elevator into her own home and bringing Mom and Dad there.

> *"What should I do with my parents' home?" she asked. "What if my dad does not get well enough to look after Mom again? How can I afford the caregivers to take care of Mom and a nursing home for Dad?"*

Susan really felt the need to get things planned out. She had 50 million questions running around in her head and was searching for the answer to each one. We scheduled a first meeting for Susan, who came in and hired us for a Life Care Plan on behalf of her parents.

Florence and Maurice are two of the growing numbers of millions of Americans for whom chronic conditions are a fact of life. The prevalence of physical and mental disability among the elderly is growing rapidly along with America's aging population. The number of Americans who suffer functional disability due to arthritis, stroke, diabetes, cancer, dementia, Parkinson's or Alzheimer's Disease is expected to increase at least 300 percent by 2049.*The challenge for our society is how we are going to manage the care of these increasing numbers of elderly persons with disabilities.

Eight years ago, I decided to devote my professional life to being an elder law attorney. Like many elder law attorneys, I initially focused my practice on Medicaid and asset protection planning. However, over the past few years I have grown increasingly dissatisfied with the answers or non-answers I was able to give to families who have questions about the long-term care system they were thrust into and did not know how to make their way through.

Our families had questions I could not properly answer: The skilled nursing facility is telling us our Mom needs this therapy and not that one — what does that mean and which one should we choose? What are Dad's housing options now that his health has improved, but he cannot return home? How do we take care of Mom during the day while both of us work? What support services are available to me as a caregiver?

These are not legal questions, but as an elder law attorney who aspired to the "holistic" approach, I needed to do better. I understood that I needed to change the way I thought about the practice of elder law. This is where the "Life Care Planning" model of practice comes in.

The Life Care Planning model places special emphasis on issues surrounding long life. The elder-centered practice incorporates traditional elder law with care management to assist individuals with chronic illness, to identify, access, and pay for good care, both now and in the future. That is not as easy as it sounds, but it is the essence of what we do. Our clients need to get good care when and where they need it, and they need to know how to pay for it.

The principal goals of the Life Care Plan that we help you develop and implement are:

1. We help make sure that you or your loved one gets good care, whether that care is at home or outside the traditional home setting, such as a nursing home. This is the most important of all goals, for it goes to the very heart of your quality of life in your later years.
2. We help you make decisions relating to your health care, long-term care, and special needs. For most of our clients and their families, it is a comfort and a relief to realize that they always have a resource of experienced, supportive, knowledgeable, and objective advisors with them every step of the way.
3. We help you find sources to pay for good care. We help protect and preserve the assets you have accumulated during a lifetime of hard work, thrifty behavior, and astute investment decision-making. We work with you through the maze of choices and options to find the best, or often, the most comfortable solution to the asset protection problem created by the need to pay for quality long-term care.

Our Geriatric Care Coordinators, who are licensed social workers, will be with the client and family every step of the way.

Since we have instituted the Life Care Planning model of practice, our office now defines our professional relationship with clients not just in terms of resolving specific legal issues, but in how effectively we assist our clients in maximizing the quality of their lives. That is truly what being an elder law attorney, in my mind, is all about.

3

THE ELDER LAW ATTORNEY
AS ADVOCATE

Our entire elder law team considers it a privilege and high honor to be able to assist the elderly and those with disabilities in navigating the long-term care system. With this privilege comes great responsibility.

As an attorney, my duty is to advocate to the best of my ability for each individual client. However, as I have previously stated, I believe there is more I can and should do. There are serious problems with access to quality long-term care. Potential future cuts to the Medicare and Medicaid programs will cause advocacy to rise in importance. I believe my duty is not to work exclusively within the existing system. I must work to change the long-term care system for the better.

The challenge is putting aside the day to day work for each individual client and figuring out where to start.

Acting is the hard part. Doing nothing is not an option. As we are in a unique position to make a difference, I believe we must act.

How do we advocate in our elder care law practice? Here are some examples:

- We were the first elder law firm in the Philadelphia/South Jersey area to have geriatric social workers as part of the elder law practice. We currently employ four geriatric care coordinators who focus on insuring that our clients receive the best possible care in the least restrictive setting.
- I am a member of the Jimmo Implementation Council. The Council is composed of Medicare beneficiary advocates, providers, and policy-makers to discuss, analyze and advance the implementation of the *Jimmo v. Sebelius* Medicare "Improvement Standard" settlement. The Council's goal is to allow Medicare beneficiaries to receive the maximum coverage for skilled nursing care. I am scheduled to travel to Washington for a meeting on March 30, 2017.
- A bill is pending in the New Jersey State Legislature to exempt up to $500 per month in gifts from being considered as part of the Medicaid five-year look back. I was involved with drafting the bill along with having the honor of testifying before the NJ State Assembly in favor of the bill.
- I led a committee on the unauthorized practice of law that resulted in the NJ Supreme Court issuing a May 2016 advisory opinion on the scope of practice of "Medicaid Advisors." While there is nothing improper with having a third party assist in the preparation of a Medicaid application for long-term care, the concern is whether these Medicaid assistance companies are engaging in the unauthorized practice of law, and therefore harming consumers.

- I traveled to the Netherlands in November 2016 as part of an Elder Law delegation to learn innovative ideas of how the Dutch provide services to those with dementia.
- On behalf of the state elder law bar, I regularly meet with state legislators and Medicaid regulators to alert them to issues affecting seniors and those with disabilities.
- We regularly present to long-term care professionals, financial professionals and attorneys to update them on changes in the law and how they can assist in advocacy of behalf of seniors.
- We sponsor a monthly caregiver support group in our office.
- We sponsor programs for seniors and veterans through the Alzheimer's Association and Jewish and Family Children's Services of Southern New Jersey.
- Our staff regularly attends national conferences and teaches other elder law firms how to engage in advocacy.

Advocacy is hard work. However, something strange happens when you decide to act to improve the lives of seniors and those with disabilities. Fulfillment and job satisfaction creep in. What can be more fulfilling than acting in accordance with the things we value most? We were given a gift, and with this gift comes tremendous responsibility and opportunity. Our goal is to continue to use this gift to make a positive difference for those we are charged with advocating for.

-4-

CAREGIVING IS HARD WORK

I have devoted the last ten years of my legal career to the practice of Elder and Disability Law. I have enjoyed every minute of counseling families with real life problems involving caring for an aging or disabled love one. I believe our office has a real impact on a family that is confronted with both the financial and emotional issues in caring for a loved one.

During these ten years, I have instructed countless clients and their families regarding asset protection planning, Medicaid eligibility, Medicare coverage, advocacy in a long-term care setting, guardianship, to name just a few topics. In order for clients and/or their children to follow my advice, they may have to take some of the following actions: contact Social Security to establish a direct deposit of the parent's Social Security check, go to the bank with a parent's power of attorney to remove a parent's name from the account, go to a funeral home to establish a pre-paid funeral account, gather five years worth of financial records and other necessary information in order to have a complete Medicaid file, obtain the necessary medical information from the doctor for a guardianship filing, meet with the nursing home or assisted living administrator to discuss problems with care.

In retrospect, I have had the easy part. My job has been simply to advise clients or their caregiver children what needed to be done in order for proper long-term care planning to occur. I did not truly appreciate the amount of work and time it takes for a caregiver to do all of what is required – until recently. In December 2007, I was called to meet Mae, a client who was a resident at a local nursing home. I was asked to meet Mae because she had no family to assist her, both financially and with care issues. Reluctantly, I agreed to serve as Mae's agent under her financial and health care powers of attorney.

For the first time, rather than advising caregivers in caring for a loved one, I was a caregiver myself. I will tell you this – it's not easy, even for someone who understands the long-term care system. Almost each day, I received medical bills and wondered why Medicare did not cover the medical service. A Medicare explanation of benefits arrived and I tried to decipher what had been paid and what had not. I have even paid a few bills that Medicare had already paid the provider. Besides visiting Mae in the nursing home, I have received calls late at night advising me that Mae had been taken to the hospital. I have had to make numerous trips to the bank to obtain needed bank statements in order to apply for Medicaid, make several trips to Mae's home in order to search for needed documents and prepare for the sale of the property, and other assorted errands for Mae when needed.

I am not reciting this laundry list of caregiving duties because I regret doing them. Actually, I have very much enjoyed assisting Mae. Assisting Mae has given me a new-found respect for how families assist our clients. When I advise a child that he or she must take certain immediate actions in order to reconfigure his or her parent's assets, I understand it involves lost time from work, lost time with family, and possible frustration at the process itself. The task itself may sound simple in theory, but the implementation process to complete the caregiving task is not a simple one.

We are here to assist you in caring for your loved one, addressing both the financial and care issues. Our job is to understand the emotional and time consuming task in being a caregiver, and help alleviate your burden. My own recent caregiving experience will not only allow me to be have more respect for families we counsel, but become a better Elder and Disability Law Attorney.

WHY I PRACTICE ELDER CARE LAW

As I have previously stated, I probably would not be practicing law if I did not practice elder care law. Eighteen years ago, once I started to explore this fascinating, challenging area of practice, I was hooked. Practicing in this evolving area of law provides a high level of satisfaction in knowing we make a positive difference in the lives of our clients and their families. However, as we deal with the day to day work, we occasionally lose focus on our mission – enhancing the lives of those elders we represent. Fortunately, we have regular client interactions which help bring our mission back into clear focus. Three recent examples are:

- A week prior to Thanksgiving, I met with a client whose husband was in a local nursing home for a rehabilitation stay following a fall resulting in hospitalization. The wife communicated that her husband wanted to come home to spend Thanksgiving Day with his family, and would be devastated if he was unable to do so for health reasons. The nursing home originally informed our client that her husband would lose his Medicare coverage for the rehabilitation stay if he went home for the day because it would be evidence that he no longer was in need of skilled nursing care. With the help of our office to advocate for the family, our client was able to go home on Thanksgiving Day to spend it with family, and returned to the SNF under a Medicare covered stay.

- Husband and wife clients both needed ongoing services and support due to dementia and a recent stroke. When we first met with the family, the husband was in a subacute rehabilitation setting, while his wife was temporarily living in a dementia assisted living community. The couple of over sixty years dreamed of continuing to live together in the same room in a long-term care setting, but the family was struggling to find the proper care setting and determining how to pay for care since funds were limited. Our care coordinator was able to secure proper housing for the couple in the same room and helped negotiate the financial arrangements in order for our clients to remain together on a long-term basis.

- I met with a husband who advised me he believed he needed to start making arrangements for placement of his wife in a nursing home. The burden of caring for his wife was becoming too much for him to handle from both a physical and emotional perspective. However, he was having a great deal of anguish in considering moving his wife of over 45 years out of the home into a safe setting. I explained to the husband that this is not supposed to be an easy decision. If you did not have second thoughts regarding your decision, something was wrong. Our care coordinator helped facilitate proper placement, making the decision easier for both spouses and the entire family.

In all three cases, health care advocacy is what made for successful outcomes. Despite their concerns about saving money, families tell us their primary goal is to promote the health, safety, and well-being of their loved one, at home, in an assisted living, or in a nursing home.

We currently have five full-time elder care coordinators (ECC). We assign an ECC to help each of our client-families with their long-term care concerns. The ECC conducts a care assessment in the client's home to identify care-related problems and assist in solving them, which might include arranging in-home help or other services or coordinating with health care and long-term care providers. When our ECCs visit clients, the assisted livings or
nursing homes know that we are in the same business: helping families take care of someone's mother, father, spouse, or other loved one. However, when necessary, our ECCs advocate and intervene on behalf of a client who is not getting proper care.

The future of elder care law lies with transforming this practice area from Medicaid asset-focused planning to an integrated care management model that elevates the elder client's quality of life and care above all other aims of the planning process.

Advocating for quality care is at the heart of what we do. This is why I practice elder care law.

-6-

DOES IT HAVE TO BE THIS COMPLICATED?

Last month, during a client meeting, I was attempting to explain to a client's family why part of the client's income must be placed into a trust in order to become eligible for Medicaid assisted living coverage in New Jersey. As I was explaining something that I knew really did not make sense to a reasonable person, I asked myself, does it really need to be this complicated?

A federal court, regarding the complexity of Medicaid law, has stated:

"There can be no doubt but that the statutes and provisions in question, involving the financing of Medicare and Medicaid, are among the most completely impenetrable texts within human experience. Indeed, one approaches them at the level of specificity herein demanded with dread, for not only are they dense reading of the most tortuous kind, but Congress also revisits the area frequently, generously cutting and pruning in the process and making any solid grasp of the matters addressed merely a passing phase."

Elder law certainly is a challenging area of legal practice. Heavy emphasis must be placed on continuing legal education, attending meetings, reviewing list serves, and constant communication with other elder law attorneys to remain knowledgeable about the ever changing regulatory field.

Just in the year 2014 alone, the following regulatory or legal changes took place affecting seniors and those with disabilities in Pennsylvania and/or New Jersey:

1. New power of attorney law in PA effective January 1, 2015;
2. ABLE Act passed in Congress allowing disabled individuals to establish savings accounts to be used for their special needs (see page 2 of this newsletter);
3. Obama Care continued implementation, including requirement that all Americans must obtain health insurance, as well as all of the exceptions to the personal mandate;
4. Medicaid expansion eligibility under Obama Care begins in NJ & a modified version begins in PA;
5. New Jersey implemented changes to its home & community based Medicaid program, now known as MLTSS (Managed Long Term Services and Supports), including moving all Medicaid beneficiaries into managed care;
6. New Jersey requiring all Medicaid long term care applicants with income above the Medicaid income cap (currently $2,199 per month in 2015) to place excess income above the cap into a qualified income trust;
7. Implementation of changes to Medicare's definition of skilled care;

8. The Veterans Administration changed their financial review process of applications for non-service related disability pension.

The above does not include the constantly changing tax laws, Medicaid eligibility figures, or future changes certain to come to both the Medicare and Medicaid programs. Our mission is to keep seniors, those with disabilities, their caregivers, and professionals educated as to the rules and how it may impact them. Is it challenging and sometimes frustrating attempting to make sense out of these complex laws? Absolutely.

That is why I find great personal fulfillment in this area of law. Myself and our staff enjoy the challenge of helping families navigate the complex, ever changing regulatory system. This is why it even more rewarding when we are able to help a family in need.

Does it have to be this difficult in navigating all the rules & regulations when caring for a loved? No, it should not be. Hopefully, Congress will finally come together in making significant changes to both Medicare & Medicaid which will make planning more user friendly.

Until then, we are here to help advocate for changes, while hopefully making things slightly less complicated. Have a wonderful and prosperous 2015.

THE FUTURE OF DEMENTIA CARE:
LET'S GO DUTCH

As an elder care law firm which places a great emphasis in health care advocacy, our goal is not to work within the existing long-term care system. Our goal is to work towards changing the long-term care system in this country for the better. We as society should be doing much more for an increasingly aging population.

With these goals in mind, in November 2016, I had the privilege traveling to the Netherlands as a member of the National Academy of Elder Law Attorneys (NAELA) delegation. The goal of the trip was to learn about how health care and legal services are provided to seniors in the Netherlands compared to the US model.

My main purpose of participating in the delegation and the highlight of the trip (visiting the Anne Frank house and the old Jewish Quarter in Amsterdam was also memorable) was the opportunity to visit the renowned "dementia village" outside of Amsterdam called Hogeweyk.

Hogeweyk is a specially designed village with 23 houses for 152 dementia-suffering seniors. There is no similar type of specialty designed dementia housing in the United States. Unlike dementia facilities in the US where all residents reside in the same type of housing, at Hogeweyk, seniors who need nursing home dementia care live in houses differentiated by lifestyle. The residents opinion on life, housing, values and standards determine their "lifestyle". Hogeweyk offers 7 different lifestyles: upper class, rural, Christian, artisan, Indonesian, cultural, and traditional.

Every Hogeweyk home houses six to eight people with the same lifestyle. People live together with other people sharing the same ideas and values in life. This makes the place where one lives a home. This lifestyle can be seen in the decor and layout of the house, the interaction in the group and with the members of staff, day to day activities and the way these activities are carried out. The residents manage their own households together with a constant team of staff members. Washing, cooking and so on is done every day in all of the houses. Daily groceries are done in the Hogeweyk supermarket. The village has streets, squares, gardens and a park where the residents can safely roam free. Hogeweyk also offers a restaurant, a bar and a theatre.

In Hogeweyk, the residents live in a place that looks and feels like home, even though it's not. What others know to be a façade, the residents see as reality, which may help them to feel normal in the midst of dementia. The question a place like Hogeweyk confronts is how much of dementia is a result of disease, and how much is a result of how we treat it? Hogeweyk has not found a cure for dementia, but it's found a path that's changing ideas of how to treat those who can no longer take care of themselves.

In the years since Hogewyk's founding, dementia experts from the United States and many other countries have flocked to the small Dutch town outside Amsterdam in the hopes of finding a blueprint for similar dementia care. While dementia-only living facilities are plentiful in the United States, none of them have offered the amenities or level of care Hogeweyk provides.

There are significant barriers, such as costs, to building a similar community in a non-socialized healthcare system, such as the U.S. However, we should do better. We must do better. Such a concept needs to be brought to the United States to reshape the face of senior care. It will take significant time, money, effort, and advocacy. We can start with the refrain, *Let's Go Dutch*.

-8-

WE NEED TO DO BETTER

"A nation's greatness is measured by how it treats its weakest members." - Mahatma Gandhi

Like many of you, I was left without words learning about the death of eight helpless nursing home residents in Florida in the wake of Hurricane Irma. It was a tragic and sad event. It is a reminder of the vulnerability of long-term care residents and older adults needing care and services in their own homes. This tragic situation provides a hard lesson about what it means to be prepared for an emergency, and the need to monitor the adequacy of those plans.

However, I believe it provides an even greater lesson for all of us. We know that elders are particularly susceptible to dehydration and heat, and therefore vulnerable in times of natural disaster like Hurricane Irma. Therefore, this tragic situation was foreseeable. Florida, federal, and local officials are investigating this terrible tragedy. The Florida nursing home disaster could have happened almost anywhere.

There has or will be lawsuits filed, with government officials blaming the nursing home and nursing home officials stating they attempted to ask government officials and the power company for help. Regardless, I believe one thing is clear – everyone failed these vulnerable nursing home residents.

We as a society have a responsibility to take care of our most vulnerable citizens. Unfortunately, after Hurricane Irma, society failed the nursing home residents. We must stand true to the above words by Mahatma Gandhi and do better to protect the most vulnerable.

We currently employ as part of our elder care law team, five geriatric social workers. Our goal is to enhance the lives of seniors we represent and engage in health care advocacy for our clients in any type of housing setting. We alone cannot prevent a tragedy like what occurred in Florida from happening again. However, we have to start somewhere.

In April and October 2018, our elder care law office will be hosting full day elder care symposiums in both New Jersey and Pennsylvania for elder care professionals. The keynote speaker for both symposiums will be Eloy van Hal, a co-founder of the Dementia Village in the Netherlands. Mr. van Hal's topic will be Dealing with Dementia: Can the Dementia Village Model work in the U.S.? The Dementia Village concept is based upon improving the quality of life for elderly people with an advanced stage of dementia by de-institutionalizing, normalizing, challenging and improving existing models and regulations. In other words, prioritizing the needs of seniors and those with disabilities as a high priority.

There is an urgent need to reassess standards and procedures for both prevention and response to emergencies. The lesson learned from the tragedy in Florida should not be that one nursing home is held to account for failing to protect its residents, or that one state takes steps to ensure that longstanding, basic resident protections are implemented for that state's nursing home residents. There is an even greater urgent need to reassess our country's priorities, and chart a positive course for taking care of our seniors and those with disabilities over the next many years.

IT'S ALL IN THE FAMILY

-9-

WHO'S IN CHARGE?

I recently met with two gentlemen who had sought my advice regarding their mother. Their situation was typical. The mother was living independently at home while her two sons were leading busy lives nearby. Although the mother was relatively healthy, she did suffer from uncontrolled high blood pressure and high cholesterol. She was not, however, what would be considered elderly—she was able to work, cook, clean, mow her lawn, garden, and participate in other activities. Then, unexpectedly, she suffered a massive stroke.

On the day of the stroke, her sons met her at the hospital. For quite some time they were unsure whether she would survive. The hospital provided excellent care, and she saw a variety of specialists and nurses. The hospital staff made sure she was stabilized and not in any immediate danger. Once she was stable, they discharged her to a rehabilitation facility.

Her sons provided what little information they had about their mother's health. They were largely unaware of her medical conditions, the medications she was taking, and any recent medical problems. Because none of their mother's medical conditions had resulted in a hospital stay or episode that would cause them concern, the mother and sons had not felt the need for the sons to be informed about her health conditions. The only person in a position to provide information to the hospital was the mother's primary care physician, and that physician was never consulted while the mother was in the hospital.

The mother's discharge from the hospital happened with almost no notice to her sons; this too is all too typical. One of her sons went to visit his mother, and it was only then that he was informed that the hospital was moving his mother to a rehabilitation facility. The sons were not given a choice regarding the facility to which she would be discharged. They also were not given any information about what to expect or to whom to talk once their mother was admitted to the rehabilitation facility.

It became obvious that the sons were still unaware of her real progress, and they did not even know what questions to ask. It was clear that they needed the help of someone with medical knowledge and knowledge of the health care system—a health care advocate.

After their mother was admitted to the rehabilitation facility, the sons tried to determine what would be the best long-term plan for her. Our Director of Care Coordinator, Janie, met with the sons and spent quite a bit of time with them to determine their goals and objectives, what they saw as the long-term plan for both their lives and their mother's life, and what would be feasible for them. Janie quickly realized that they had no idea of their mother's capabilities since the stroke, where she was in the rehab process, and her prognosis. The sons had tried to ascertain this information— they spent time with their mother during normal working hours while taking time off from their jobs.

They tried to speak with the physical therapist, but that person was never available, so the sons obtained opinions from anyone to whom they could speak. They never were able to speak with a physician, they never met any type of director, and they never received any real answers.
Know what questions to ask.

Janie was able to interpret the information they provided, and she gave them an honest assessment of what their mother's needs were at the time. She began to ask questions such as: "Was your mother's primary care physician consulted?" "Has your mother been seen by a neurologist since she left the hospital?" "What has the psychiatrist said about her progress?" "Who was present at her team meeting?" The questions she asked boiled down to one question, "Who was in charge of leading your mother's medical team and who was in charge of pulling everything together?"

In a perfect world, the mother's primary care physician would remain in charge. Unfortunately, our medical system is fragmented and that does not always occur. The second choice for the person in charge is someone in the family. In the situation described here, the sons were unaware of any of their mother's health condition. In addition, they had no medical knowledge, they did not know what questions to ask, and they did not know to whom they were supposed to pose their questions. They were under the impression that progress reports such as "Your mother is improving" were standard. Janie asked the right questions, and she pointed out that the question "Who is in charge?" was the most important question.

As a result of their conference, the sons discovered that their mother had not been seen by the necessary specialists. Janie gave the sons a realistic view of their mother's capabilities and what she would be able to accomplish with further rehabilitation. With this information and with the assistance of a gerontologist, the sons have come up with a plan to bring their mother home with assistance. She has been given the opportunities she needed to rehabilitate as much as possible, and Janie was able to help arrange the right type of in-home care. This has been overseen by the gerontologist acting as the team leader in conjunction with her new primary care physician.

The lesson to be learned from this example is that the medical system is fragmented. While it may seem that a loved one is getting the right type of care, only an expert and an advocate can point out what is missing. Our office's Geriatric Care Coordinators are here to assist your family so that you never have to ask the question "Who is in charge?"

-10-

PLANNING TO REPLACE THE
IRREPLACEABLE PARENT

We spend a good part of our day helping families navigate the long-term care system to secure care for a senior. Many families do not realize that we also assist in planning for the families of seniors. Most parents of children with disabilities are aware of the necessity to plan financially for such a child; however, they may not have considered living and care arrangements for their child, regardless of the child's age. Some families realize the need for such planning but do not want to face the parents' inevitable aging and death. Such a "head in the sand" approach can ultimately be traumatic for the child with disabilities.

Recently, we have worked with several families in which an aging parent has a medical crisis that leaves the parent in need of long-term care. Prior to needing long-term care, however, the aging parent was the primary care provider for an adult child with disabilities. Once appropriate care is secured for the aging parent, particularly if the care is in a facility, then the crisis of the child's care begins.

In many of these cases, the child has been disabled since birth and has been living with the parent. The parent has always been the care provider, so the adult disabled child may not be receiving any type of public benefits or community services, and this child may not have been involved with any other care providers. When the parent is no longer available, either because of illness or death, the child is not only faced with losing the parent as a primary care provider, the child may also face the dilemma of leaving the only home the child has ever known. Such life changing transitions are difficult for any child, but for the child with disabilities these transitions can be traumatic. When the parent has a medical crisis or dies, some type of transition will be inevitable and necessary.

In some of these situations, families can make temporary arrangements for the adult child with disabilities to live temporarily with the child's other family members until they can find a more permanent solution. It is stressful for the individual with disabilities; this individual is now removed from both the care of the individual's beloved parent and also the individual's familiar environment. This individual is also placed into the chaos of someone else's life.

In the worst case situations, there are either no family members living in the local area, or none who are able to provide adequate care. Therefore, there is an immediate crisis for the child with disabilities for both the short-term and long-term. In order to avoid such a crisis, it is critical for the parent of a child with disabilities to devise a plan for that child's care in the event the parent can no longer be the caregiver.

There are several planning objectives that parents of children with disabilities should pursue. The first objective is to ensure that the child is receiving as many benefits and services as possible. Some available benefits, such as Medicaid waiver programs, have long waiting lists and people may be on the lists for years. There may be programs available in the community through the community services boards as well as local recreation centers. Many parents have followed their natural instincts to shield their child with disabilities. In many cases, however, if it is possible for the child to be involved in a sheltered work program or community activities, the child may become more independent than initially thought possible. If the child has a relatively high level of independence, then there may be more community alternatives and housing options available. The parent will also want to ensure that the child's health care benefits will remain intact at the parent's death.

Another planning objective involves assessing housing options in case the parent is no longer available to be the primary caregiver. If the child will be living with siblings or other family members, then in many cases it is a good idea for the child with disabilities to spend time with the potential caregivers in the caregiver's home before a crisis occurs. This can make the eventual transition easier and more comfortable, and the person with disabilities is more likely to thrive in the new environment. The situation is more difficult if the child with disabilities will not be living with family members if the parent becomes ill or dies. Families should consider transitioning the child to the new environment (such as a group home) while the parent is still available. The parent can then monitor the transition to the new environment and ensure that the child is receiving the care that the parent desires. This also gives the parent the peace of mind that the child will not have to experience the disruption that can occur at the parent's illness or death.

Each family's situation is different; however, they all share one thing in common: the need to adequately plan to transition care for their family members with disabilities. Planning for the inevitable certainly provides the best result for everyone.

-11-

CAN I GIVE YOU A HUG? ABSOLUTELY!

Recently, I met with Michele regarding her mother, Helen. Michele was referred to our office by the admissions director at the nursing home where her mother currently resided.

Michele and I spent about 90 minutes together in our firm's conference room. During our time together, Michele confided in me her concerns that her mother would not be eligible for Medicaid to cover her mother's nursing home care and that Michele and her husband were at risk to be financially responsible for any outstanding charges being due.

Michele went on to discuss her mother's health and living arrangements over the past five years. Approximately five years ago, due to her mother's deteriorating health, Michele and her husband agreed to have mom move into their home. Two years into the move, as Helen's health continued to deteriorate, she became wheelchair bound. For over two years, Michele was her 24/7 caregiver on many days, causing her to miss significant work time. Michele bathed, dressed, and prepared meals on a regular basis for her mother, as well as went shopping and took her mom to all doctors' appointments. Her goal was to keep her mom at home and avoid nursing home placement.

Helen, like many of our senior clients, is a very proud individual, and did not want a free ride. Therefore, Helen gave her daughter $25,000 as well as paid her a monthly rent because she said "you are the only one taking care of me." Some of these funds were used to renovate a bathroom to make it wheelchair accessible.

Unfortunately, as Helen's health continued to deteriorate, nursing home placement was unavoidable. Thinking that she would qualify her mother for Medicaid since her mom was under $2,000 in total assets, Michele went innocently to the local Medicaid office to apply for nursing home Medicaid coverage. Michele was shocked when the Medicaid caseworker told her that her mom would not qualify due to the previous alleged uncompensated gifts and that Michele had to give her mom all the money back in order to qualify.

Why did Michele care for her mom for five plus years prior to nursing home placement? Because she thought is was the right thing to do. She witnessed the care and dedication her parents gave her grandparents, and she thought it was necessary to do the same for her mom. She was completely shocked by the Medicaid caseworker's matter of fact statement that she would need to give all the money back.

I sat quietly as a listened to Michele's story as I felt and heard the concern and angst on her face and in her voice. I then advised her how I believe we can assist her in qualifying her mother for Medicaid in such a fashion that neither she nor her husband would be responsible for any

outstanding nursing home bill. As the tears rolled down Michele's face, I witnessed the anxiety being lifted from her. As I accompanied her to our parking lot, she said to me, "If it was appropriate, I would hug you right now."
Wow! That is what elder law is all about. I love this job.
Our entire staff is very fortunate to do what we do. Whether we are meeting with a caregiver child, caregiver spouse, or the elderly client, we get the opportunity to help relieve their anxiety, to give them peace of mind. While we help the client, the client also helps us. They expose us to an appreciation of a humanity we discover in ourselves that we may not have understood or felt before – and could not, except for them.

In case you were wondering – *we love hugs.*

-12-

BUILDING A SUKKAH CREATES
LASTING FAMILY MEMORIES

For the past several years, including this year, my family and I have built a Sukkah in our backyard to commemorate the fragile dwellings in which the ancient Jews dwelt during their 40 years of wandering in the desert after the exodus from slavery in Egypt. A Sukkah is a temporary hut constructed for use during the week-long festival of Sukkot. It is topped with branches and decorated with autumnal, harvest or Jewish themes. We eat our meals in the Sukkah during the seven days of Sukkot, which took place the last week of September.

Having a Sukkah in your home is an important Jewish custom, but the process of building the Sukkah is, to me, the most valuable experience. Our nine-year-old son, Gregory, loves to build. He helps me with putting up the Sukkah's walls and roof.

Our three other children (not including baby Aitan) assist with decorating and adding lighting. Yes, building the Sukkah can teach important lessons about Jewish heritage and history. However, the process of building can create family bonds and memories that last a lifetime. My wife and I receive great joy watching our children work together to decorate the Sukkah.

This concept certainly does not just apply to Jewish customs. For example, I am sure that choosing a Christmas tree and decorating the tree can generate equally lasting memories.

When clients and their children come to our office, we attempt to learn about them from more than just what their estate planning documents, bank accounts, or current health status tell us. It is the life experiences to date built on family customs that really show who this person sitting across from us truly is. Although their current destination is what they or their family is in our office to discuss, I try to elicit some information about their journey to their current destination.

The journey to a destination is where the learning and lasting memories are created. Whether it is building and decorating a Sukkah with your family, choosing and decorating a Christmas tree, or the journey called life, memories can be created that will have a positive impact upon all who are part of the journey.

-13-

FATHERS AND CHILDREN

Father's Day typically gets outshined by Mother's Day, at least if you compare the two days based upon consumer spending. A Father's Day gift you may want to consider is the new nonfiction book, "Pops", by Pulitzer Prize winning author, Michael Chabon. "Pops" is a collection of seven essays on fatherhood, each of which shines a light on moments revealing the plight of the modern father.

The book began life in 2016 as an article in GQ Magazine for which Chabon was dispatched to write about Paris men's fashion week. He took his youngest son, Abe, with him on the assignment as a bar mitzvah present. Abe was 13 at the time and, thanks to his older brother, was already deeply into clothes, though he had long superseded his sibling in terms of style, knowledge and enthusiasm. In the essay, Chabon takes the role of Abe's "ponderous old minder", amused at what he saw at fashion week as models prowled the catwalk in shaggy yellow Muppet pants. By the end of the week, he was none the wiser about fashion, but he was much wiser about his son's obsession.
Chabon in his essay writes:

> *You are born into a family and those are your people, and they know you and they love you and if you are lucky they*

even, on occasion, manage to understand you. And that ought to be enough. But it is never enough. Abe had not been dressing up, styling himself, for all these years because he was trying to prove how different he was from everyone else. He did it in the hope of attracting the attention of somebody else—somewhere, someday—who was the same. He was not flying his freak flag; he was sending up a flare, hoping for rescue, for company in the solitude of his passion.

You were with your people. You found them.

As a parent you hope your sons or daughters will find an obsession to consume them. The trick is attempting to let your children find their own way.

At the end of the essay, Chabon's son admits that of all the fashion shows they attended during their week in Paris, his favorite was the one that he went to alone. He tells his father that the best part was the people. "They get it.". Abe had found his tribe.

As the father of five children, I originally believed that our job was to have our children learn from us. In reality, our job may simply be to learn from our children. Happy Father's Day to all the dedicated fathers.

-14-

AITAN ELI ROTHKOFF
WELCOME TO THE WORLD

"Teach your children what you believe in. Make a world that we can live in."-Crosby, Stills, Nash and Young

June 28, 2010 was a very special day for our family. That day was the birth of our fifth child and third son, Aitan Eli Rothkoff. Although this was our third birth experience (we have two sets of twins), in some ways, the experience was all new. Both sets of twins were born nine weeks premature. As such, they were immediately intubated and rushed to the neonatal intensive care unit where they remained for five weeks until they were healthy enough to come home.

This time, though, my wife and I held baby Aitan immediately after birth, and were able to take him home upon my wife's hospital discharge. As our other children are now nine and twelve, we were able to share as a family the precious new gift we received.

That said, I do not expect to win any father of the year awards. Without my wife doing an amazing job in juggling maintaining the home, managing the kids' busy schedules while running her own business, I do not know where I would be today. At first, when my wife told me she was pregnant, I was quite apprehensive. Did I want to change my lifestyle on account of the new baby at the age of forty-two? The answer thus far is a resounding yes! In just a few weeks, I have seen the joy baby Aitan has not only brought to my wife and me, but to our children and grandparents as well. Yes, our lifestyle will need to change for a short while. We cannot just hop in the car or stay out late with the kids. That is a small price to pay for a lifetime of joy.

In some ways, in addition to a normal childbirth, fatherhood just feels different this time around. I think that has a great deal to do with the nine year gap between our second set of twins and Aitan.

Last month, while driving, I stumbled upon an interview on NPR with Dan Gottlieb, a psychologist, newspaper columnist, and radio talk show host. He was explaining how a severe auto accident several years ago that left him paralyzed actually helped to improve his outlook on life. He stated that his permanent injuries provided him a sense of emotional relief because it left him no choice but to "be the man I want to be, not the man I think I should be."

Similarly, the time span between children has given me a different outlook on fatherhood and life in general. Nine years ago, I was working to build an elder and disability law practice and attempting to balance my work life and family life. Although a constant struggle, I now feel comfortable with my role as a father and husband.

In Hebrew, Aitan means "strength." Our wish for Aitan is that he has the strength to overcome the obstacles that life will invariably place in front of him to lead a life of fulfillment and happiness.

-15-

FIVE KIDS AND FIVE DOGS: SAY WHAT??

One year ago my wife and I purchased a vacation home in the Poconos. A key thought of buying the home was the needed excuse to travel two hours on occasional weekends to spend time together as a family without the distractions of birthday parties, carpools, Little League games, and other activities that control our usual weekends.

My wife and I just celebrated our 15 year anniversary. If you had asked me 15 years ago if I could have imagined we would have 5 kids and 5 dogs, I would have replied there would have been a greater chance that I would be the starting shortstop for the Philadelphia Phillies. Well, life brings many twists and turns, the latest of which occurred Labor Day weekend.

We spent Labor Day weekend at our Poconos home. On Saturday morning, I had a meeting scheduled with attorneys in Stroudsburg, PA., which was having a street festival on its Main Street that day. We went as a family to my meeting so my wife and kids could walk around Main Street to visit the festival vendors and have lunch. As fate would have it, directly on the sidewalk in front of the law office was the local animal shelter with two pugs in a cage.

My wife immediately turned to me and said, "We are taking them home."

My first instinct was to say there was no way that we would add two more pugs to our family when we already had three at home. That was before I heard the pugs' story. The two pugs had been at the shelter for one week. Their owner, an 86-year-old man, had passed away a week earlier. His family then dropped the dogs off at the local shelter. The pugs were age 7 and 8 respectively, with the 8 year old having only one eye. The shelter staff advised that since the pugs have been together so long, they would have to be adopted together.

After hearing the story, I thought for a minute. The only reason we were on Main Street in Stroudsburg that afternoon was so I could meet with other attorneys to assist them with an elder law matter. The pugs were in a cage because their elderly owner died and they had no place to go.

Sometimes it seems as if there is a higher force at work that you must obey. Two hours later, we were driving back to South Jersey, five dogs in tow.

We try to teach our children to assist those less fortunate than them. We encourage them to volunteer their time, many hours of which involve helping seniors. This was a way of helping both the deceased owner as well as the dogs themselves. How could I resist?

However, even I have some limits. We only have room in our bed for three dogs, otherwise I am on the couch. The two new pugs, Coco and Gigi, sleep in our daughters' beds. Five kids and five dogs? Do the Phillies need a 43-year-old shortstop?

-16-

LOVE LOST

*"Love begins with a smile, grows with a kiss,
and ends with a teardrop."* — Anonymous

As is the nature of an elder and disability law practice, I usually meet our client or his or her spouse at a time when at least one spouse has deteriorated in health to the point of needing some form of long-term care. In some cases, a spouse has recently passed away or during the course of our representation, a spouse passes away. In most cases, the clients have been married for many years, usually over 50 years.

I attempt to not only understand the husband and wife's present situation, but also to obtain a background on their family and personal history. Although I cannot possibly fully understand the grief the client is going through regarding their recent loss, I at least have a better understanding about the couple's shared life experiences together.

I believe mourning the death of a spouse is different than mourning the loss of a parent. After the children have moved away and have children of their own, a spouse's death leaves an emptiness that is hard to fill. My father died at age 56 in 1997. Although I think about him every single day, my sister and I were able to come home each day to our spouse and children. My mom was left with an empty house and wonderful memories. There was no one in the house with whom to share the events of the day, discuss the broken pipes and rotten politics, relish the antics and achievements of children and grandchildren. Who will open the jar that defies efforts, close a stuck window, hold the ladder to change a light bulb, split wood for the fireplace, take the wheel when the other spouse is too sleepy to drive? I recently had an experience with a client that moved me to tears. I represent an elderly gentleman who currently is in a local assisted living community. He had lost his wife of over fifty years about six months earlier. He and his wife met while he was in the service in the 1950's, stationed in Germany. Although they never had children, they traveled all over the world and built a wonderful life for the two of them.

I recently met him at the bank to view his wife's jewelry that he had purchased for her over the years, contained in a safety deposit box. We spent over an hour together in a small room at the bank while he took the jewelry out of the box piece by piece, describing when and for what purpose he had purchased each piece. As he took each piece out, he lovingly kissed each one. It was my privilege to spend that time with him as he honored his late wife.

As he kissed each piece, I thought to myself, "Wow, how can I possibly attain and maintain the love that obviously he and his wife shared for over fifty years?" That is the type of spousal relationship we all attempt to achieve. Many of our client's spouses suffer from Alzheimer's or other forms of dementia, and have been deteriorating in health for quite some time. The healthy spouse has had the opportunity to be the main caregiver for several years prior to the spouse's death. Even in that situation, the loss of a spouse can be devastating. In many ways, the healthy spouse being the primary caregiver gave meaning to that spouse's life. A client whose wife recently passed away due to complications from Alzheimer's Disease said to me, "although caring for my wife the past few years was difficult, my wife gave meaning to my life." As the poet Alfred Lord Tennyson said, "Tis better to have loved and lost than never to have loved at all."

SPORTS & LASTING MEMORIES

-17-

BASEBALL: UNITING THE GENERATIONS

"The game of baseball has always been linked in my mind with the mystic texture of childhood, with the sounds and smells of summer nights and the memories of my father." — Doris Kearns Goodwin

The first official game at the Phillies' new ballpark, Citizens Bank Park, is scheduled for April 12, 2004. I therefore thought the beginning of a new era for baseball in Philadelphia would be a perfect time to digress from the usual elder law topics, and instead write an article about baseball.

Those who know me well understand I have three main passions in life: my family, elder law, and baseball. This article will encompass all three of these passions.

Typically, a caregiver child who has increasing difficulty in dealing with the financial, emotional and medical issues involving an ailing parent contacts us for assistance. The caregiver child is distraught at watching the once active parent succumb to dementia or Alzheimer's disease and is torn by the potential for nursing home placement. In many cases, the parent may not come to the initial consultation.

However, as an elder law attorney, my client is always the elderly parent. Therefore, I always visit the client in his/her home, assisted living residence or nursing home. Upon visiting the client, my first goal is to make the client comfortable with me. I begin to talk about what he/she did for a living and what his/her hobbies are. Invariably, especially in the case of male clients, we begin to talk baseball. If the client grew up in Brooklyn, we talk about the old Brooklyn Dodgers and Ebbets Field. In this fashion, I am better able to understand the relationship between father and son/daughter. I attempt to use baseball as a mechanism to bring the family together during a possible crisis situation.

Similarly, my father, Leonard Rothkoff, taught me to love the game of baseball. My father died in 1997 at the age of 56. Some of my fondest memories of my father surround the game of baseball. My dad was a baseball purist. He insisted on keeping score at every game he took me to at Veteran's Stadium. I will always remember our trip to the Baseball Hall of Fame when we each saw our respective childhood idols, Richie Ashburn and Mike Schmidt, inducted into the Baseball Hall of Fame. I still remember as if it were yesterday our embrace sitting in the 700 level at the Vet after the Phillies won the 1993 Pennant against the Atlanta Braves.

About two weeks before my father's death, in anticipation of his 57th birthday, I attended a baseball card show in which Robin Roberts, the Phillies Hall of Fame pitcher, was signing his new book on the 1950 Philadelphia Phillies. I had the book autographed by Robin Roberts as a birthday present for my dad. Unfortunately, I never had the opportunity to give him his present. However, that book will always be linked to the wonderful memories of my father.

I am sure that many of you have had similar experiences with your parents. Each of you bring your wonderful memories of your parents to our office. I enjoy practicing elder law because it allows me to make a difference in an individual's life while keeping those precious memories alive and well.

On April 12, opening day, I will have walked into Citizens Bank Park for the first time. Right by my side will be my father, scorecard in hand.

-18-

THE GLOVE

I am writing this article a week after the Jewish High Holy days and the Pope's two day visit to Philadelphia. The past week has been an opportunity for self reflection and inspiration hearing the Pope's words of wisdom. However, you do not necessarily need to wait one year for Yom Kippur or a generation for the next Pope visit to Philadelphia. You can gain inspiration and self reflection by looking at everyday objects all around you.

We all have cherished memories of loved ones that a personal object helps bring to life. My dad died 19 years ago at the age of 56. As a child, I spent countless hours pitching to him in our backyard, which, in my eyes, was my field of dreams. As I reached my teenage years and my velocity increased, my dad had to place padding in his glove so his hand would not become sore.

My dad's fifty some year old baseball glove now sits proudly in my office. When I need to make a difficult decision or simply am having a difficult day, a grab my dad's well worn glove from a shelf and I put the glove on my left hand, pumping the glove with my right hand. The glove gives me inspiration and strength to come to the right decision and helps strengthen my resolve. I immediately harken back to my field of dreams with my dad being 45 feet away from me (our backyard was too small to be at regulation distance, 60 ft. 6 in. apart).

My dad was also an avid collector of American Presidential political campaign buttons and American stamps. As a kid, I marveled at how my dad was so meticulous in making sure that every stamp was in perfect condition and cutting the plastic stamp holder to just the right size. Unfortunately, our current house suffered a fire about 15 years ago. The fire badly damaged the stamps and political campaign buttons.

For the past fifteen years, due to the soot and dirt caused by the fire, the stamps and buttons have sat in trash bags in our garage. I have not thought too much about either until recently. My daughter, a high school senior, is studying the 1950s in American history. She was given an assignment of compiling artifacts from the 1950s. She asked me if I had any objects she could use for her school project. I immediately knew what she could use. I went to the back of the garage and opened the trash bags full of the political campaign button albums. I was covered with soot all over my hands and clothes, but I did not care. I knew exactly what I was looking for – the "I like Ike" Dwight Eisenhower buttons from the 1952 Presidential campaign. Interestingly, of the 9 albums containing political campaign buttons ranging from 1900 thru the Reagan era, the 1950's album was the only album that was not damaged by the fire. Sadly, my children never met their grandfather. With the help of the buttons, they have the opportunity to gain a glimpse of who he was and what he meant to the family.

Sometimes you gain inspiration when you least expect it. Last month, I attended the funeral of a client. The client's only family member was a 59 year old daughter with special needs. Due to the daughter's developmental disability, she has been living for the past many years in a nearby group home. I served as our client's agent under her power of attorney since she had no other family or friends able to serve. Nine people attended the funeral, five of which were from our elder law office. The daughter asked such beautiful, profound questions to the rabbi which no one else would have the courage to ask – "Will I see my mom tomorrow? Will my mom call me like she always does at 7 PM tonight? Do you feel anything when you are dead?

It was a beautiful tender moment of sincere love. No matter how an individual comprehends loss, the loss is genuine and profound. However, the memories will always remain.

Whether it is a baseball glove, buttons, or simply closing your eyes and remembering your loved ones, seeking inspiration from deceased loved ones helps you gain renewed strength to tackle the challenges that life may present.

-19-

OPENING DAY AND A BAT-MITZVAH:
IT'S ABOUT RITUALS

Our daughters, Liza and Julia, celebrated their Bat-Mitzvah on April 2, 2011. We celebrated following the formal service at our synagogue with a dinner dance. The food and the band were fantastic.

However, what stands out in my memory from that wonderful day were our daughters standing on the bimah reciting Hebrew blessings that our ancestors have recited for thousands of years. My wife and I could not have been prouder of our daughters on this special day.

The Jewish religion, like other religions, is about ritual. There is a certain sense of comfort in these religious rituals being passed down from generation to generation. There are religious rituals at the time of death that bring comfort to all who mourn.

Rituals do not only take place in the religious arena. The day before our daughters' Bat-Mitzvah, our daughter Liza and I attended the Phillies' opening day game. Baseball has many rituals associated with the grand old game. The singing of the National Anthem, the seventh inning stretch, singing "Take Me Out to the Ball Game," eating peanuts and cracker jacks, attempting to catch a foul ball, are among many other rituals. These rituals are passed down from generation to generation, from parent to child. Another ritual between fathers and sons is playing catch. I will always remember pitching to my dad almost every night in our backyard during the little league season. I still can picture the mound of dirt in my backyard where grass used to be that I used as a pitcher's mound. My sons and I carry on this ritual today.

A Bat-Mitzvah symbolizes a Jewish child's passage into adulthood. During my dinner dance speech to our daughters, I tried to explain to them that like the Phillies opening day of the season, today was their opening day into Jewish adulthood. However, unlike the Phillies goal of winning the World Series, life is not about winning the World Series. Life is not about a destination. Life is about the journey.

During their journey, like baseball, they will commit errors, strike out, and ground into double plays. There will be happy times and not so happy times. Through both the good and the not so good, they will grow as a person and be better individuals from their experiences.

Through it all, life is about sharing experiences with family members and friends, with many being experienced through the use of rituals. Whether a religious ritual or the religion of baseball, rituals unite us from generation to generation. When I walk in the door from work in the evening, I am typically asked these magical words, "Dad, do you want to have a catch?"

-20-

PURE FANTASY

"Got a beat-up glove, a homemade bat and brand-new pair of shoes? You know I think it's time to give this game a ride. Just to hit the ball and touch 'em all — a moment in the sun; it's gone and you can tell that one goodbye!"
—John Fogerty

I have always dreamed of playing baseball in the big leagues. For one nostalgic week, I got a chance to realize my dream. In January, I traveled to Clearwater, Florida, along with my good friends, Michael and Jeff, to the Philadelphia Phillies Fantasy Camp. For one week, we played on the fields and dressed in the locker rooms that were used by Phillies greats such as Richie Ashburn, Robin Roberts, Steve Carlton, and Mike Schmidt. Every time I entered the locker room and put on the Phillies uniform, I felt like Shoeless Joe Jackson in the movie "Field of Dreams." I kept asking myself, "Is this heaven?"

For those who are unfamiliar with what baseball fantasy camp is, fantasy camp is an opportunity for the average baseball fan to rub elbows with some of their childhood or adult heroes. It's a chance to spend a week playing baseball with your favorite team or sports personalities in great facilities. Your playing level does not matter as much as your desire to have a good time.

Getting the opportunity to play alongside some of your childhood and adult heroes was absolutely fabulous, but I will most remember the people I met and played alongside for the one memorable week. Regardless of age, running ability, arm strength, or bat speed, 140 fantasy campers were united in their love of the game of baseball and our fantasy of being kids again.

I had the most respect for the retirees who made the pilgrimage to Clearwater. People like 68-year-old Ed, a retiree from Arizona, and former Philadelphian. At the end of the camp, Ed could barely move. Regardless, Ed was living his fantasy and having a great time just being out on the field playing with other campers, some of whom were 30 years younger. However, I most remember Ed for asking me on the first day of camp whether I knew Leonard Rothkoff, my father. My father, who died 10 years ago at the age of 56, taught me to love the great game of baseball. Ed and my dad went to Temple University Pharmacy School together. I immediately felt a kinship with Ed, as if Ed was there, at that very moment, for simply more than his own fantasy.

Or 71-year-old Charlie "Shoehorn," a teammate of mine on our team, the Mudhens. Baseball is known for individuals with colorful nicknames, and Charlie is one of them. On the first day of camp, Charlie was wondering why his foot hurt him so much. After playing in his cleats all day, he finally figured out the reason — he had a shoehorn in one of his cleats. Like Ed, Shoehorn could not run. Regardless, he was there, sore foot and all, due to the love of the game.

Forty-two-year-old Chuck was a teammate and the most valuable player on the Mudhens, the worst of 10 teams at camp, with a 0 -7 record during the week. With all due respect to Chuck, being the MVP on the Mudhens was equivalent to Richie Ashburn being the MVP of the 1962 New York Mets, arguably the worst team in Major League history. Chuck's wife and sister, the Mudhen's lone cheering section, accompanied Chuck to Clearwater. I met all three approximately a year earlier when I represented their grandmother, whom they were struggling to care for in their home. We instantly bonded, talking about baseball and the Phillies.

Regardless of your age, you are never too old to have fun and attempt to be a kid again. In January, 140 of us did so on the ball fields of Clearwater, Florida. You can live your fantasy any way you choose.

As if by fate, fantasy camp ended on January 28, 2007, on what would have been my dad's 67th birthday. It was a great day to end a week of pure fantasy.

-21-

THE SUPER BOWL'S EFFECT ON UNITING GENERATIONS

My wife, a very intelligent women, is not a big fan of sports. She intends to go out for dinner during the Super Bowl and could care less about watching our hometown Eagles hopefully beat the Patriots to win their first Super Bowl. However, for many others, the Super Bowl or other big sporting events have a powerful meaning.

The Super Bowl has virtually turned into a national holiday. Certainly, around Philly, it is "the" event of the year. Regardless of whether you are a fan of football, baseball, basketball, soccer or hockey, I find the beauty of sports is their uncanny ability to unite the generations.

Some of the fondest memories of my deceased father involved baseball. I will always remember our trip to the Baseball Hall of Fame when we each saw our respective childhood idols, Richie Ashburn and Mike Schmidt, inducted into the Baseball Hall of Fame. I will also cherish the memory of the spring training pilgrimage to Clearwater, Florida with our sons.

Football played an important role in my relationship with my grandfather Harry. Harry was an immigrant from Poland who came to America in his late teens in order to escape anti-Semitism. He spoke English with a heavy accent. He learned to become a tailor in America. After retirement, he worked part-time on weekends in the basement of our house. Some of my favorite memories of my grandfather were in the 1970s watching Eagles games with him on Sundays in the basement of our house while he was busy on his sewing machine. As an eight year old, I was attempting to the best of my eight year old ability to explain the rules of American football to him. I am not sure he truly understood the rules, which may have been partly my fault. Regardless, having the opportunity to bond over football was priceless to an eight year old.

So *"fly Eagles fly, on the road to victory"* and enjoy making cherished memories with your family.

REFLECTIONS BY
JEROLD E. ROTHKOFF, ESQ

-22-

REFLECTIONS: HOW I TURNED
TO ELDER LAW

It has been exactly five years since I opened the doors to my own Elder Law firm. As I look back, I am reminded of the events that forever altered the course of my professional career. For the first five and a half years of my career, I had been practicing in the area of general civil litigation, with an emphasis in creditors' rights and personal injury law, when I became involved in an elder law matter.

The matter involved a spouse being sued for her husbands alleged outstanding nursing home bills. As I began to investigate the case, I became aware that I needed to become much more familiar with Medicaid and nursing home laws to provide the proper representation for my client. Coincidentally, I subsequently learned that the National Academy of Elder Law Attorneys was having its annual 1999 spring conference in Philadelphia.

With my interest piqued, I signed up for the conference not knowing what to expect. Within the first two hours at the conference, I became energized in a way that had eluded me in my first years in the practice of law. I got home that night (since the conference was local) and advised my wife that I wanted to change my practice area. I knew back then that there was something about this field of elder law that would fulfill me in ways which I never could have imagined when I went to law school and set out upon my journey to become a lawyer. Two hours at the conference changed my life.

One early case that I handled left an indelible impression on me and characterizes the essence of what elder law attorneys do for their clients. It involved a woman who suffered from Chronic Obstructive Pulmonary Disease (COPD).

Medicare denied her coverage for a procedure called Lung Volume Reduction Surgery. At that time, in order for Medicare to pay for the complicated and risky surgery, the patient must have enrolled in a national trial program under Medicare. Once enrolled in the trial program, half of the patients received the surgery, while the remaining half were randomized for continued therapy, which, in essence, was a death sentence. My client was randomized for continued therapy, and therefore Medicare would not cover the cost of the approximate $50,000 surgery. She did not have the financial means to pay privately for the surgery, and therefore, on her behalf, I appealed Medicare's denial. Through my research and investigation, I learned of a world-renowned cardiothoracic surgeon in St. Louis, MO, who pioneered lung volume reduction surgery. With his assistance, my client won the administrative hearing, meaning that Medicare would cover the clients' surgery.

There are no words for the gratification I felt when I was able to explain to this family that I could help them. It is a feeling that I will never forget. My client and her family thanked me, stating that she can now dream of the possibility of playing with her grandchildren for the first time, something that she could not previously have done due to her breathing difficulties. For the first time in my career I felt that I had a real impact on a family that was confronted with real problems. In an instant, life meant something more to me. I had become a problem-solver, and it felt good. It still feels good today.

Unfortunately, due to my client contracting pneumonia, she died before she could travel to St. Louis for the surgery. However, at the time, we received the second known administrative decision in the U.S. that overturned Medicare's denial of lung volume reduction surgery. We were able to share our decision with several other individuals across the U.S. who were confronted with the same issue. Ultimately, in early 2004, due to overwhelming medical evidence regarding the benefits of lung volume reduction surgery, Medicare decided to cover the surgery. I like to think that my client had some small role to play in Medicare's decision.

As I look back on these past five years, I have probably learned more from my clients than they have learned from me. The most important thing I have learned is to listen. Listen to the clients' wonderful stories about the wars they have fought, the places they have been, and the people they have met. We have much to learn from the elderly and disabled, and they have much to share.

It has been an honor and privilege assisting seniors, the disabled, and their families these past five years. It is a debt of gratitude that I can only hope to repay.

-23-

A GOOD MAN AND A FEISTY WOMAN

Alan Feinberg with grandson, Gregory, as an infant.

On Christmas Day 2009, my wife received a call from my mother-in law that her father, Alan Feinberg, was being taken to the emergency room at Virtua Marlton Hospital due to shortness of breath. After a few days of diagnostic testing, Alan was diagnosed with terminal lung cancer. Three days after being admitted he was placed on a ventilator. He was subsequently transferred to the Hospital of the University of Pennsylvania on a ventilator. The oncologists advised our family of the options available to treat the significantly advanced lung cancer. None were good. Our family made the excruciatingly difficult decision to remove the ventilator. Twelve days after entering the hospital without knowing he had terminal cancer, at the age of 68, Alan Feinberg was dead. He died peacefully on January 6, 2010, surrounded by his loving family. He left his loving wife, Janice, his daughters, Erica and Pam, a brother, and five grandchildren. Several hundred family and friends turned out to pay their respects at his funeral.

While my father-in-law was being rushed to the emergency room, on the same day, about 5 miles away, I received a call from Cadbury Nursing Home in Cherry Hill, New Jersey, that our client, Mae, was found unresponsive in her nursing home bed and was being rushed to the emergency room at Kennedy Hospital in Cherry Hill. Since I was Mae's health care representative under her health care power of attorney, I traveled to the emergency room at the hospital to find Mae on a ventilator. Although Mae had a few close friends and neighbors, she had no other family. I felt it my obligation to stay with her. I stayed for about an hour, under the belief that I would need to make a decision regarding the withdrawal of life sustaining treatment for Mae, age 95.

I called the hospital the next day to find, much to my pleasant surprise, that Mae was taken off the ventilator and moved to intensive care. Mae had congestive heart failure and had been back and forth from the nursing home to the hospital for the past few months. I spoke with the intensive care nurse who had advised that Mae's prognosis was poor. I subsequently spoke with Mae about what she would want to happen should she be placed back on the ventilator, which the nurses believed would happen in the near future. Her response to me was — "What don't you understand, I want to live!" She went back and forth from the hospital to the nursing home a few more times over the next subsequent months. A day after her 96th birthday, on March 11, 2010, Mae passed away peacefully at the nursing home. She was survived by an estranged son. Her funeral was attended by her few close friends and neighbors. One of her close friends gave a beautiful eulogy. Unfortunately, Mae's estranged son did not attend his mother's funeral.

Alan and Mae's vastly different paths in life intersected on December 25, 2009. Alan was a successful stockbroker, married to Janice for 40 years, during which time they raised two wonderful daughters and had five loving grandchildren. At the time of his passing, he was the president of a no-kill animal shelter in Lindenwold, NJ, in which he pursued his life's passion, rescuing animals and finding them safe homes.

I had known Mae for about four years prior to her death. She was living in her own home. I was asked by the social worker at the nursing home to assist Mae with her finances and health care decisions since she has no one else. She had a few wonderful friends and neighbors who looked after her, but no family to assist her. I did not know a great deal about Mae's life prior to her life at the nursing home. However, if she had something on her mind, she told it to you without sugarcoating it. She clearly had a zest for life and attempted to live life to its fullest.

Regardless of their vastly different backgrounds and family, Mae and Alan did have similar traits. They both had very strong personalities. Alan and Mae did things on their terms, regardless of what anyone said.

However, they did diverge on their ability to control their destiny at the end of life. Neither Alan nor his family had time to prepare for his illness. Although his family was at his bedside at the time of his passing, he could not communicate his wishes about whether he wanted to live in that condition. Mae communicated her wishes to me loud and clear, passing away on her own terms.

Regardless of the number of friends and family one has at the time of one's passing, the value of an individual's life is measured by the impact he or she has had on others. Whether you have a few close friends or dozens of close friends and family, one's impact on others can be equally important. Mae and Alan, in different circumstances, have left a positive legacy and impact on those closest to them.

-24-

THE MEASURE OF OUR SUCCESS:
ONE HUG AT A TIME

As I write this article, I am sitting in a Kansas City, Missouri hotel room attending the 2nd annual conference sponsored by the Life Care Planning Law Firm Association (LCPLFA). Approximately one hundred elder law attorneys and social workers are meeting to discuss substantive issues and practice management concerns related to the Life Care Planning concept of an elder and disability law practice. The mission statement of the LCPLFA is as follows:

> ...to develop life care planning as a holistic legal practice which anticipates and provides legal and care advocacy services to the firm's clients as their circumstances and health care needs change. Members are committed to helping clients and their families navigate the long-term and health care system and advocate for good care during their loved one's journey through the elder care continuum.

It has been approximately two years since we adjusted our practice focus to concentrate on Life Care Planning by incorporating the use of a geriatric care coordinator into our practice. Thus, we not only concentrate on traditional elder law practice areas, estate planning, eligibility for public benefits, etc., but now emphasize maximizing the best possible care for our clients, whether in or out of the home. When meeting with clients and their families for the first time, I emphasize that they are not retaining our office specifically for a power of attorney or to obtain valuable long-term care benefits. They choose to retain our office to assist them in navigating through the long-term care maze that they did not willingly enter. What they are purchasing is a long-term relationship between the client, their family, and our office. I advise clients at the first meeting that I expect myself and my staff to receive at least one hug from the client or client's family member during the course of our representation. Our job is to alleviate the burden on caregivers caring for a chronically ill or disabled loved one.

Receiving a hug from a client or caregiver symbolizes to us that we helped to alleviate the burden placed upon them. A recent client meeting helps to illustrate this point.

Janie Deleon-Male, our Geriatric Care Coordinator, and I recently met with a husband and wife and their children concerning the wife's need for care. The family explained to us their concerns and their mom and wife's current situation. The mom and wife suffered from a rare form of Alzheimer's Disease. The family's goal was to attempt to keep their wife and mom at home for as long as possible. We explained the Life Care planning concept to them and emphasized the concept is based upon the relationship that develops between our firm and the client and their family. The wife and mother was very unsteady on her feet.

Nonetheless, at the end of the initial meeting, on her own, she attempted to get up from her chair. Everyone in the meeting jumped out of their seats to attempt to steady her. However, as soon as she was steadied, she said to me,

"I give you a hug." It was one of the most memorable hugs I have ever received.

We look forward to receiving many more hugs from clients and family members. Thanks for helping to measure our degree of success.

-25-

A SPIRITUAL JOURNEY ON AGING

As an elder care lawyer for almost 19 years, I have learned the importance of studying health care delivery systems, specifically related to the delivery of services to seniors. There is no doubt the U.S. health care system can and should improve the health care services provided for an increasingly aging population.

In November 2016, I had the privilege of traveling to the Netherlands as a member of the National Academy of Elder Law Attorneys (NAELA) delegation. The delegation's goal was to learn about how health care and legal services are provided to seniors in the Netherlands compared to the U.S. model. As an outcome of the trip, our office has scheduled Eloy van Hal, the co-founder of Hogeweyk, the world renowned Dementia Village outside Amsterdam, to travel to New Jersey in April 2018 to speak about the Dutch model for treating individuals with dementia.

Given the enlightening experience studying the Dutch long-term care system, I wanted to experience more. From February 16-26, 2018, I was part of a group of 18 professionals from the U.S. who traveled to Israel to focus on aging in Israel. Among tour participants were chaplains, clergy, rabbis, a doctor, and a geriatric care manager.

The Israel tour was significantly different than the Netherlands tour for several reasons. First, I was the only attorney on the tour. In the Netherlands, we were all attorneys, and therefore we tended to ask similar questions and analyze the issues in similar patterns. The Israel tour, in contrast, was comprised mainly of chaplains who concentrated on end of life issues with an emphasis on spirituality. As a result, I obtained a greater appreciation of the value of spirituality at the end of life that I intend to apply to my elder care law practice in the future.

Additionally, unlike the Netherlands, in which I had no previous connection to the country, the Israel tour became highly personal. While I was on a journey about aging, the trip soon became an exploration into myself. In addition to exploring at least a dozen different aging services in Israel for both Jews and Arabs, I had the opportunity to meet many of my distant cousins, had dinner with a childhood friend in Tel Aviv, and had a chance meeting with a gentleman in a coffee shop who I believe was placed there by a higher being at that exact time for me to meet.

I met Jay Pollack at a coffee shop in Jerusalem. Jay was originally from Philadelphia who moved to Israel in 1967. As it turned out, he knew my great-grandfather, Pinchas Rothkoff, who died before I was born. He remembered Pinchas having a tailor shop on South 4th Street in South Philadelphia. As a 10-year old, Jay remembered him to be the leader of Sabbath Saturday morning services in South Philadelphia in the late 1940s. He recalled Pinchas as always bossing people around during the service which intimidated Jay. Jay's father told him that my great-grandfather would receive complaints

from women every day of the working week that their
dresses were too tight or didn't fit well. Therefore on the
Jewish Sabbath, Pinchas deserved to be king. Sometimes
people are put in certain places for a reason.

The substantive tour itself taught me that regardless of
the country, the work across different societies responds to
the different needs in every place and time, but the
principles are the same. I had a precious opportunity to see
how government and society in Israel interact in conducting
the fight to ensure a life with dignity for elders. I witnessed
how some problems are being solved and how many
problems still remain. Israel's problems are certainly
different from our problems in the United States—it is a
much younger society, divided between Jews and Arabs,
and with modern and very conservative actors of society
living side by side, not always in peace. The responses in
Israel are sometimes different from those in the U.S., but
surprisingly they are many times the same as here. We have
so much to learn from them and they have so much to learn
from us. Ultimately, we fight this fight together wherever
we are.

What seems to me to be a major difference is the effort
in Israel to pay specific attention to personalizing
individualized care and management as much as possible. I
also learned that excellent caregiving across the continuum
can occur in physically substandard buildings if there are
really good caregivers.

My journey ended on a highly spiritual note at Ben
Gurion airport outside Tel Aviv. After passing through
security, as I walked to the airport gate for my return flight
to Newark, I noticed a man outside an airport gift shop
putting gift packages on a table. Being a curious individual,
I stopped to inquire what the packages were for. He

proceeded to explain in English with an Israeli accent that the gift packages were Shalach Manos, gifts of food that are sent to family, friends and others on the Jewish holiday of Purim. I assumed there was a charge, but he said they were free, so I graciously took a gift bag (forgetting of course that I should not accept packages from anyone prior to boarding a plane). The very nice gentleman went on to explain that he was distributing the free gifts to give to someone you love to tell them the story of Purim, the triumph of good against evil. The Shalach Manos Purim gifts were sponsored by the families of three Israeli teen boys, Gil-Ad Shaer, Eyal Yifrah, and Naftali Fraenkel, kidnapped and murdered by terrorists while coming home from school in 2014. The gentleman who handed me the gift bag was Ofir Shaer, the father of Gil-Ad Shaer, who was 16 when he was murdered. I was stunned and speechless. I gave him a hug and walked to my gate. I sat down in the airport terminal and began to cry. My spiritual journey had come to an end and another was just beginning.

-26-

MAKING A DIFFERENCE

We wish all of our friends and clients a very happy and healthy New Year. In this New Year, I urge you to reach out to seniors and those with disabilities. Don't be hesitant to volunteer your time to help those in need. It can be volunteering at a local senior center or nursing home or taking an elderly relative whom you have not seen for a while to lunch or inviting him or her over for dinner. You would be surprised at the impression you would make on the recipient of your good deeds.

A few months ago, I spoke to residents and family members of a local assisted living facility. Since the talk was in the early evening, I asked my identical twin nine year- old daughters, Liza and Julia, if they were interested in joining me. They quickly jumped at the opportunity to figure out why dad would want to spend two hours at an assisted living facility.

Liza and Julia assisted me in distributing a folder to each attendee. Some of the residents were so excited by my daughters' presence that they felt the urge to give them each a hug before they left for the evening. In the car on the way home my daughters commented on how excited they were that they were able to put a smile on the residents' faces.

Recently, it was disclosed that former Chief Justice Sandra Day O'Connor's husband, suffering from Alzheimer's disease, had a romance with another woman. Contrary to the expected reaction, the former justice was thrilled to see her husband of 55 years so happy and content.

Was Justice O'Connor's reaction unnatural, or is it something we should all strive for? We hear the adage that we never want to become an old married couple. Well, maybe being an old married couple is not such a bad thing. Making sacrifices for someone you care about has immeasurable rewards.

We, in our Elder and Disability Law practice, strive to act for the betterment of our senior and disabled clients. We attempt to treat each client as if he or she were family by maintaining the elder's dignity. We attempt to assist our clients in a variety of ways.

We may be visiting a client in his or her home to assist the family with long-term care placement or making the home safe for their loved one to remain at home. We may be counseling a wife who needs to place her husband in a nursing home and is concerned about protecting her assets from long-term care costs. We may be counseling children whose parent desperately needs institutional care but is unwilling to go there voluntarily and doesn't understand how serious the situation is. We may work with a married couple that has an autistic child in obtaining guardianship and establishing a special needs trust to protect their special needs child. We may represent an elderly individual who was subject to improper financial exploitation. My daughters were shocked that such a simple act as visiting seniors can make such a difference. Not only will you make a positive impact on seniors, your act will also have a positive impact on you.

-27-

THE MEASURE OF OUR SUCCESS:
OUR RELATIONSHIPS WITH OUR CLIENTS

As I write this article, I am sitting by my wife's side while she lies in a hospital bed recovering from a high fever and an infection. We have already heard terminology used such as she is under "observation status" and her assigned physician is a "hospitalist." We also have spoken with her physician discussing what may have caused the high fever and the status of different blood cultures attempting to locate any infections. (She is feeling fine now).

For a layperson, including myself, dealing with the health care system can be a frustrating experience. We rely upon the medical expertise of those health care professionals who are treating us. However, often we feel lost inside the health care system not knowing what questions to ask, what options there are for treatment, when we can refuse a specific type of treatment.

For our clients and their caregivers, in the majority of cases, concerned about future long-term care options, it can be a particularly daunting experience. In addition to the health care itself, they need to be aware of the options available for future care as well as the resources available to pay for the care. Our health care system does not do a very good job with educating patients as to their long-term care options.

For over a decade, our elder care law firm has been members of the Life care Planning Law Firm Association (LCPLFA). Two years ago, I had the privilege of serving as the Association's president. The mission statement of the LCPLFA is as follows:

> ...to develop life care planning as a holistic legal practice which anticipates and provides legal and care advocacy services to the firm's clients as their circumstances and health care needs change. Members are committed to helping clients and their families navigate the long-term and health care system and advocate for good care during their loved one's journey through the elder care continuum.

It has been over ten years since we adjusted our practice focus to concentrate on Life Care Planning by incorporating the use of a geriatric care coordinator into our practice. We not only concentrate on traditional elder law practice areas – estate planning, eligibility for public benefits, etc., but place an emphasis on maximizing the best possible care for our clients, whether in or out of the home.

When meeting with clients and their families for the first time, I stress that they are not retaining our office specifically for a power of attorney or to obtain valuable long-term care benefits. They choose to retain our office to assist them in navigating through the long-term care maze that they did not willingly enter into. What they are purchasing is a long-term relationship between the client, their family, and our office.

I sometimes advise clients at our first meeting that I expect myself and my staff to receive at least one hug from the client or client's family member during the course of our representation. Our job is to alleviate the burden on caregivers caring for a chronically ill or disabled loved one. Receiving a hug from a client or caregiver symbolizes to us that we helped to alleviate the burden placed upon them. A recent client meeting helps to illustrate this point.

I recently met with a husband and wife and their children concerning the wife's need for care. The family explained to us their concerns and their mom and wife's current situation. The mom and wife suffered from Alzheimer's Disease. The family's goal was to attempt to keep their wife and mom at home for as long as possible. We explained the Life Care planning concept to them and emphasized the concept is based upon the relationship that develops between our firm and the client and their family. The wife and mother was very unsteady on her feet. Nonetheless, at the end of the initial meeting, she attempted to get up from her chair on her own. Everyone in the meeting jumped out of their seats to attempt to steady her. However, as soon as she was steadied, she said to me, "I give you a hug." It was one of the most memorable hugs I have ever received.

We are here to help you navigate through the health care and long-term care system. We look forward to receiving many more hugs from clients and family members. Thank you for allowing us to assist.

-28-

SUNDAY WITH SINATRA (AND MY DAD)

December 12, 2015 would have been Frank Sinatra's 100th birthday. My dad loved Frank Sinatra. I vividly remember as a child driving on Sunday mornings with my dad in his Oldsmobile 98 listening to Sid Mark and Sunday with Sinatra. As a young child, I did not understand how my dad could enjoy that type of music. Back in the 1970s, there was no escape from the Oldsmobile and Sinatra, as I did not have an iPhone, iPad, or satellite radio at my disposal. However, as I have aged, I actually have grown fond of Sinatra's music. It may have to do more with remembering the quality time I spent with my dad than actually enjoying the music, but hearing "You Make Me Feel So Young" always brings a smile to my face.

Bruce Springsteen will be 100 years old in 34 years. Bruce Springsteen is my equivalent of my dad's love affair with Frank Sinatra. During our family car rides, instead of Sunday with Sinatra, it is E Street Radio blasting from the car audio system. Our five children do not understand (neither does my wife) why I love Bruce so much. They think Springsteen is country music. At least they have their iPhones and iPads to listen to.

Currently, Sinatra is played regularly in assisted living and nursing home communities. In year 2050, can you imagine Born to Run and Badlands being played in long term care communities? Study after study has shown that music has power – especially for individuals with Alzheimer's disease and related dementias. Music can shift mood, manage stress-induced agitation, stimulate positive interactions, facilitate cognitive function, and coordinate motor movements.

Music also has the power to unite generations. Last year, our twin daughters and I traveled to Brooklyn, NY for the 2014 Rock and Roll Hall of Fame Induction Ceremony and Concert. I was there to see the E Street Band (absent Clarence Clemens and Danny Federici) inducted and our daughters were there to witness Nirvana's (absent Kurt Cobain) induction. It was a night I will always remember, made most memorable by sharing the evening with our daughters.

Perhaps one day, our children will hear Born to Run, and smile thinking about their dear old dad. How does "Sunday with Bruce" sound?

-29-

BOBBY THE PUG: LIFE LESSONS LEARNED

"We can judge the heart of a man by his treatment of animals." — Immanuel Kant

In February 1994, I met two very special individuals. The first was my future wife, Erica, who I have been privileged to be married to for over ten years. The second was a very special pug dog named Bobby, who just happened to be owned by Erica. Bobby died on August 5, 2006. During the twelve years Bobby was in my life, Bobby taught my family and me more about life than I could ever have imagined.

Bobby was not your average dog. Bobby was a special needs dog. He was born with a neurological impairment that limited his ability to walk. He had to be carried up and down steps, and usually fell on his face or back after taking several steps. Due to this, we, at times, walked him in a baby stroller.

Nonetheless, regardless of Bobby's limitations, he was a fighter. He learned how to compensate for his difficulty walking and more or less was able to get where he needed to go. He also attempted to keep our other two dogs in line by biting at their legs or whatever he could hold on to. Gradually, over the years, Bobby's disability worsened. It became more and more difficult for him to walk, necessitating the need to carry him from place to place.

During his last few years, he was unable to ambulate on his own. At first, I was not looking forward to caring for this disabled pug. I never had a dog before and dreaded the thought of all the extra work that taking care of Bobby called for. Amazingly, it turned into a labor of love. For almost eleven years, my day began and ended with Bobby in my arms. Each morning, I carried him down the steps and outside to "make." This routine was reversed each evening prior to bedtime.

The gift Bobby gave myself, my wife, and our children, was the ability to care for someone who needed our help. We enjoyed being able to help him. Bobby helped show us that caring for another in need has its own immeasurable rewards. In a way, Bobby gave more to our family than we ever gave to him.

I work with elderly clients whose sole source of companionship is their pet. They refuse to leave their home for independent or assisted living because no one will care for their pet. These clients not only have a companion, they also have someone that is dependent upon them. Someone they are responsible for. The loss of their pet will also entail the loss of their ability to give.

For twelve years, Bobby gave my family and me the ability to give. For that, we are forever grateful. Goodbye, my dear friend; your life lessons will be put to good use.

-30-

MY TEN-YEAR EDUCATION

In December 2008, Clifton B. Kruse, of Colorado Springs, Colorado, one of the most respected Elder Law Attorneys in the nation, died. We are all poorer for the loss. Clifton, a prolific writer, wrote "Selma's Cat and Other Things That Matter" (subtitled "A Lawyer's Intimate Conversations With His Elder Clients"). "Selma's Cat" grew out of a series of short essays he wrote about actual clients, how to understand them, how to discover what is important to them, and what they really mean.

I am beginning my tenth year as an Elder & Disability Law Attorney. Clifton's death allowed me to reflect on what I have learned during my ten years working with seniors, those with disabilities, and their families. Here are my top ten things I have learned:

10. Although protecting assets is important for clients, getting the best care always comes first.
9. Always listen to your clients and their families before you talk.
8. Being an advocate for seniors and those with disabilities gives you an opportunity to do well by doing good.

7. Family always comes first, be it your own family or the client's family.

6. Give yourself an opportunity to learn from your clients who have years of wisdom and experience to share.

5. Our country does a lousy job of caring for those chronically ill and disabled.

4. A loving family is the greatest form of wealth anyone could have.

3. The people and staff you surround yourself with make you a better person.

2. The morals my parents have instilled in me helped shape my goals in life and facilitated my commitment to spend my professional life helping seniors and those with disabilities.

And finally...

1. The unwavering guidance, support, and encouragement of my wife, Erica, has allowed me to be the very best I can be.

Although I have learned a great deal in ten years, I have yet to graduate. I have much more to learn. I am eternally grateful to our clients and their families who have allowed our office to assist them during the past ten years. These past ten years are a commencement, not a graduation.

-31-

TEN YEARS OF PERSONAL FULFILLMENT

February 2010 will mark the ten-year anniversary of the Law Offices of Jerold E. Rothkoff. I could not have imagined, on February 1, 2000, where the law firm and myself would be professionally today. The Rothkoff Quarterly has and continues to be an outlet to express my thoughts and desires, specifically related to caring for loved ones with chronic illnesses. I have attempted to write about real life events that people can relate to. During the ten-year period, I have written about, among other topics, caring for our disabled dog, the death of my father and grandmother, multiple articles on caring for a loved one, and of course, baseball, particularly related to using baseball as a means to unite the generations.

Our daughters, Liza and Julia, were born in 1998. As a means to support my family while my wife stayed home with our newborn twin daughters, I explored the potential of opening my own law office. Given the previous experience with my grandmother, as well as the ever-increasing age of our population, I thought Elder Law was an area that was ripe for growth. However, at first, the thought of opening my own office was simply a means of putting food on the table for our growing family. Unexpectedly, it has turned into my calling.

In early 1999, I attended an Elder Law conference in Philadelphia. Within the first two hours at the conference, I became energized in a way that had eluded me in my first years in the practice of law. I knew back then that there was something about this field of Elder Law that would fulfill me in ways which I never could have imagined when I went to law school and set out upon my journey to become a lawyer. Two hours at the conference changed my life.
For the first time, I had become a problem-solver, and it felt good. It still feels good today. We are privileged to get the opportunity to guide families in a time of crisis in order to get the best care possible while determining how to pay for expensive care. It is a responsibility that we take quite seriously.

Of course, like any business, we have had to evolve and change to adapt to the marketplace and client's needs. In 2005, our firm adopted the "Life Care Planning" practice model by incorporating social work to assist families in advocacy for their loved ones. Life Care Planning has enabled us to truly provide "holistic" services that our clients need and deserve.

Most importantly, I could not have grown professionally and personally by myself. I have learned that you are only as good as the people you surround yourself with, and I have had fantastic people by my side on this wondrous   journey.
To our staff—Janie, Stephanie, Joanne, Yona, Jennifer, Elizabeth, Jane, Rita, Lori, Susan, and Lois— thank you for everything you have done, and your commitment to seniors and those with disabilities.

Thank you to my family— my wife, Erica, and children, Liza, Julia, Evan, and Gregory (and number five due in June 2010)— who always have encouraged me to be the best I can be, as well as get me back on course when I sometimes veer in the wrong direction.

Lastly, a huge thank you to our referral sources, clients, and their families with whom we have had the opportunity to work. It has been an honor and privilege assisting seniors, the disabled, and their families. I look forward to many more years together.

-32-

OUR 15TH YEAR ASSISTING SENIORS & THOSE WITH DISABILITIES

We are celebrating our 15th year assisting seniors and those with disabilities. In November, we completed our move of our South Jersey office to a larger location. The move to a significantly larger office will allow us to continue to expand the elder and disability law services we offer our clients and their caregiver loved ones.

As I have previously written, I did not begin my career as an elder law attorney solely because I had a passion for helping seniors. I originally decided to become an elder law attorney for a very basic reason – to support my growing young family. However, once I started to explore this fascinating, challenging area of practice, I was hooked. For the first time in my career I felt that I had a real impact on a family that was confronted with real problems. In an instant, life meant something more to me. I had become a problem-solver, and it felt good. It still feels good today.

As an elder law attorney, we distinguish ourselves not so much by asking "What happens when I die?", but more importantly, "What happens if I live?" Especially as we see our clients living longer while coping with a variety of physical, medical and legal challenges. Therein the journey lies. Frequently, we accompany our clients and their families on the "journey" that may last several years with circumstances frequently changing along the way.

Practicing in this evolving area of law provides a high level of satisfaction in knowing we make a positive difference in the lives of our clients and their families. As I look back on the past fifteen years, I have probably learned more from my clients than they have learned from me. The most important thing I have learned is to listen. Listen to the clients' wonderful stories about the wars they have fought, the places they have been, and the people they have met. We have much to learn from the elderly and disabled, and they have much to share.

I recently read a published interview of John Bogle, the founder and former CEO of Vanguard, the mutual fund company. He was asked what advice he would give his children regarding their careers. He said he would advise three things: 1) family comes first; 2) never forget the value of luck and where you have come from; and 3) never, never, never say you did it all yourself because no one ever does it all themselves.

I want to thank my parents for instilling in me the value of giving back to others. I want to thank my wife, Erica and our five children for always knowing at the end of the day, I can come home to their love and support. I have had the opportunity to be surrounded by great people over the years, within both my personal and professional life. Thank you for making me a better person each and every day.

It has been an honor and privilege accompanying seniors, the disabled, and their families on their journeys these past fifteen years. It is a debt of gratitude that I can only hope to repay.

LESSONS IN STORYTELLING

-33-

DUELING TESTIMONY - SETH ROGEN VS. BEN AFFLECK - A COMMENTARY ON LONG-TERM CARE IN AMERICA?

It was an interesting day in Washington, D.C. on Wednesday, March 5, 2014. Two Hollywood celebrities testified at separate U.S. Senate subcommittee hearings at the same time regarding two different topics.

Actor Seth Rogen offered touching and sometimes funny remarks that detailed his mother-in-law's struggles with Alzheimer's disease. Rogen testified on behalf of the Alzheimer's Association to advocate additional federal funding and research for Alzheimer's disease and related dementia. While Rogen's testimony was powerful and put a light on a topic that should be discussed more often, there was one major problem: Only two senators among eighteen stuck around for the 6-minute testimony. That's right, 16 senators either didn't attend the session or left before Rogen spoke.

The actor called them out on Twitter, writing, "Not sure why only two senators were at the hearing. Very symbolic of how the Government views Alzheimer's. Seems to be a low priority."

In fact, one of those that left, Sen. Mark Kirk of Illinois, even took a photo with Rogen before doing so, later thanking him for speaking out via Twitter. Naturally, Rogen asked him why he didn't stick around to hear what he had to say. Kirk said he had another meeting to attend, but watched the testimony later. Rogen and his wife have launched an organization, Hilarity for Charity, to help educate young Americans about the disease.

In another Senate hearing room in the same building, Ben Affleck testified on the dire situation in the Congo before the Senate Foreign Relations Committee. Affleck testified in front of a packed house, with most Senate committee members present.

Affleck has visited the central African country nine times since 2007. Four years ago, the actor started his advocacy organization, Eastern Congo Initiative, dedicated to helping bring peace and prosperity to the region. He told the senators that while Congo is more peaceful than when he first visited the region 11 years ago, it remains at a crossroads.

It is my understanding that the situation in the Congo has been unbearable, involving mass rapes and killings. However, I am admittedly not very knowledgeable about the current state of affairs in Congo. Perhaps I should be. However, I can tell you what affect Alzheimer's disease and related dementia has on our country. These affects include:

- Total payments for health care, long-term care and hospice for people with Alzheimer's and other dementias are projected to increase from $203 billion in 2013 to $1.2 trillion in 2050.

- Dementia care accounts for a larger portion of health care costs in the US than cancer care.
- Alzheimer's disease is the sixth leading cause of death in the United States. Deaths from Alzheimer's increased 68% between 2000 and 2010, while deaths from other major diseases, including the number one cause of death (heart disease), decreased.
- Alzheimer's is the only cause of death among the top 10 in America without a way to prevent it, cure it or even slow its progression. *Source: www.alz.org*

There has to be room in this world to bring attention to both of these causes along with so many other issues that plague our world. However, we have enough problems right here at home, and the care we give our elderly should be right at the top of that list.

Each person can focus on what becomes important to them – then hopefully we can collectively make this world a better place. To quote the late great Pete Seeger– "Participation– that's what's gonna save the human race." As long as we participate in something – disease prevention, genocide awareness, human rights, let us all just continue to stand up for what we believe in.

-34-

MY GRANDMOTHER THE TEACHER

My grandmother, Fannie Weiss, died in 1999 as the result of end stage Alzheimer's Disease. Towards the end of her life, she was unable to recognize family and friends. I remember her fondly for her love of Yiddish humor, dancing, and singing, as well as her fondness for taking every Sweet'N Low packet home with her from each and every diner in Northeast Philadelphia.

She loved to show off her grandchildren to her friends and take us to her community pool. She was always there for me, as well as her other grandchildren when needed. Yet, when she needed me the most, at the end of her life, I was unwilling to be there for her.

Although this is something I will always regret, I have attempted to turn the lesson learned by the events surrounding my grandmother's death into a positive experience. A lesson I attempt to incorporate each and every day into both my professional and personal life.

Fannie died in a nursing home surrounded by no one. Once she lost her cognitive ability, I rarely, if ever, visited. I figured why bother visiting if she did not know who I was nor remember if I was there. In retrospect, it was a purely selfish act on my part.

Why spend the time visiting with someone who would not remember you were present? Because it does matter. I have recently returned from Chicago attending the annual conference of the Life Care Planning Law Firm Association. The keynote speaker was William H. Thomas, M.D., a noted innovator in the field of long-term care. Dr. Thomas spoke of the need to develop a new lifecycle described as "Elderhood." In Elderhood, elders are a respected part of the community where others come to enjoy what aging has to offer. Today's society, instead, neglects and relegates elders so that they become invisible at a time when they have something special to offer the larger culture.

Regardless of her mental abilities, my grandmother deserved to have family and friends comfort her and provide companionship when she was most vulnerable. Due to the perceived lack of something to offer, I relegated Grandmom Fannie as "invisible."

Life lessons, in most cases, do have a positive result. People ask me — why did you become an elder law attorney? My answer – Grandmom Fannie. Our Elder and Disability Law office is about to celebrate its tenth anniversary in January 2010. My staff and I continually strive to advocate for seniors and those with disabilities so they are not deemed to be invisible, and are an important part of our society.

In the end, unexpectedly, Grandmom Fannie did teach me an important life lesson. It is wisdom I try to put to work each and every day.

-35-

UP, UP, AND AWAY!

In my ten years in writing and publishing this Newsletter, I have yet to write a movie review — until now. If you have not already done so, do not walk, kindly run to see the movie, *Up*. The title is deceptively simple, which is fitting, because the movie from Pixar Animation is deeper and more complex on every level than it would initially appear.

It is a mismatched buddy comedy, the buddies being a curmudgeonly 78- year-old man and an 8- year-old boy, who wind up together in a flying house, traveling to South America. Between the richness of the characters and their interactions, it will not take you long to forget that *Up* is a cartoon and become immersed.

A life-altering meeting

We begin some 70 years before, when Carl Fredricksen was just a boy, worshipping the glamorous explorer Charles F. Muntz. Even then, Carl moved with the quiet cautiousness of an old man — that is, until he meets the energetic tomboy Ellie, who brings out the fun he never knew he had inside him. *Up* shares their decades-long romance in a lovely, poignant montage. It lasts just a few minutes without a single word spoken, but it tells a full and satisfying story. Do not even bother holding back the tears: They will come, and deservedly so.

From there, though, there is nowhere to go but up, literally. Now a crusty widower facing eviction and an antiseptic life in a retirement community, the former balloon salesman ties thousands of helium balloons to his house and soars into the clouds. His eventual destination: Paradise Falls in Venezuela, where he and Ellie always promised each other they would go. Carl has an unexpected passenger on his voyage: Russell, an overeager Junior Wilderness Explorer who had knocked on Carl's door hoping to earn the final badge he needs to become a senior scout: assisting the elderly. They make an unlikely but lovable pair: the rigid Carl and the cheerful Russell. Their bond is sweet, their journey joyous.

The beauty of *Up* is its message about the perils and promises of aging, and its ability to strike an emotional chord that floats across any demographic divide. Kids will like it; but it will deeply touch adults.

So many people find themselves grasping tightly to the past, holding onto things as if they were holding onto life. But things are not life. Remembering the past is good – it reminds us of how we came to be who we are. But clinging to the past is death, even if you are still alive.

In *Up*, what turns Carl around is the sense that he still has something to do. He was going nowhere, but when circumstances intervened, he found that he was going somewhere. Carl thinks that the answer to his life's malaise is a trip to Paradise Falls to keep his final promise to his wife. But what he discovers is that his life's value is not merely in what has gone before, but what is still to come. In this case, Carl is rejuvenated when he fights a new battle, sets off on a new adventure.

As people get older, they see less and less of life before them, so they are tempted to retire from active pursuits and, instead, chase and hold fast to what has passed. We yearn for our glory days, replaying our golden moments while present opportunities slip by.

We strive in our office, through our holistic Elder Law practice, to allow our clients, whenever possible, to continue to live in the present. We love to hear our client's stories of how husband and wife met or raising their children. However, we attempt not to allow our clients to cling to the past. Our goal is to bring out the "Up" in each and every client.

-36-

A LIFE WELL LIVED

Last month, our long-term client, Bob, passed away. At the beginning of our representation, we emphasize to the client or family that our goal is building a relationship with the client. We do not typically assist a client in an individual transaction. Our goal is to help the family navigate the issues involved with long-term care and follow the client & their family along the elder care continuum (home care, adult medical day care, independent living, assisted living, and/or nursing home care) as the care needs increase.

We worked with Bob and his family longer than we have worked with any other client during my 15 years as an elder law attorney. Bob first contacted our office about 13 years ago regarding his mom. We assisted him with care issues related to his mom, and eventually qualified her for nursing home Medicaid coverage. About 6 years after his mom died, Bob contacted our office once again in regard to his wife's Alzheimer's diagnosis. We worked with Bob and his wife, Eileen, with financial and estate planning, and eventual nursing home placement for Eileen. Bob's wife passed away about 3 years ago. Approximately two years ago, Bob's son contacted us regarding his dad's deteriorating mental condition. Unfortunately, Bob had developed dementia and was in need of assistance. We once again assisted the family with financial and long-term care placement issues, designing an asset protection plan and eventual assistance with assisted living placement.

I read that famed singer and songwriter Leonard Cohen recently celebrated his 80th birthday. He celebrated by smoking a cigarette. Although I am not recommending taking up smoking at any age, Leonard Cohen had an interesting idea. Jason Karlawish, MD, a professor of medicine at the University of Pennsylvania, in his New York Times editorial published September 20, 2014, asked an interesting question – When should we set aside a life lived for the future and, instead embrace the pleasures of the present?

Our country is becoming more and more obsessed with preventing diseases. Our office's geriatric care coordinators spend hours documenting the multiple medications our clients are taking. Our clients and or caregivers sometimes complain that their days are spent going from one doctor to the next. Prevention of disease is important, but at what cost? As Dr. Karlawish writes, a national investment in communities and services that improve the quality of our aging lives may be necessary. Most people desire not simply to pursue life, but also happiness.

Medicine is important, but it is not the only means to achieve happiness.

Bob was a very proud and learned man who enjoyed life. Although he certainly had his difficult days caring for his mom and his wife, and eventually himself, he never lost his boyhood enthusiasm for life. He always had a positive outlook on life regardless of the circumstances.

Bob was a fatherly figure to me. He witnessed first hand the growth of our elder law firm and he always had words of wisdom regarding my elder law practice or life in general. Thank you to Bob and his family for allowing us to assist them on the journey for the past 13 years. We have much to learn from both Bob as well as Leonard Cohen.

EPILOGUE

The doors to our Elder Law office opened in January 2000. During the past two decades, I have attempted to chronicle my experiences helping families navigate the legal and care issues involving the aging process. During this time, I hope our Elder Care Law team has made a small difference in improving the lives of those we are charged to advocate for. I thank all of our clients and families that have put their trust in the Rothkoff Law Group.

I started my career as an Elder Law attorney. The addition of healthcare advocacy in 2006 has allowed our Elder Law firm to transition from traditional elder law to an Elder "Care" Law Firm. I have now become an Elder Care attorney, a title I wear very proudly.

ABOUT THE AUTHOR

Jerold E. Rothkoff, a practicing New Jersey and Pennsylvania attorney, is the Principal of the Rothkoff Law Group, where he dedicates his practice to serving clients in the areas of elder law, life care planning, asset protection, veterans benefits, estate planning, and long-term care advocacy.

Jerry Rothkoff has been, and continues to be, an outspoken advocate for the rights of the elderly and disabled. He writes for and gives presentations regularly to attorneys and other professionals about elder law. He is a frequent lecturer, speaker, and author for the Pennsylvania Bar Institute and the New Jersey Institute for Continuing Education, as well as non-profit and professional organizations. He is the former co-host of SeniorTalkRadio on AM 860 WWDB. He has made numerous other radio and television appearances in which he discussed legal rights of the elderly.

Jerry is the author and founder of the Rothkoff Quarterly, a newsletter of current news and issues concerning the elderly and disabled. He is also the author and editor of the South Jersey Guide to Senior and Disability Resources and the Southeastern Pennsylvania Guide to Senior and Disability Resources.

He is Past President of the NJ Chapter of the National Academy of Elder Law Attorneys, and Past President of the Life Care Planning Law Firm Association. He is also the former Chair of the New Jersey Bar Association Elder and Disability Law Section.

Community activities include being a member of the Board of Directors of the Jewish family and Children's Services of Southern New Jersey (JFCS) and Artz Philadelphia. He also is involved with the Alzheimer's Association, as well as numerous other advocacy groups.

Jerry Rothkoff is a 1986 graduate of Syracuse University. He obtained his Juris Doctor degree in 1993 from the Widener University School of Law, and began work at a Philadelphia, Pennsylvania law firm. In February 2000, he opened his own elder care law practice.

Outside of his elder law practice, Jerry and his wife, Erica, keep busy with their five children.

JEROLD E. ROTHKOFF, ESQ.

Made in the USA
Middletown, DE
01 July 2021